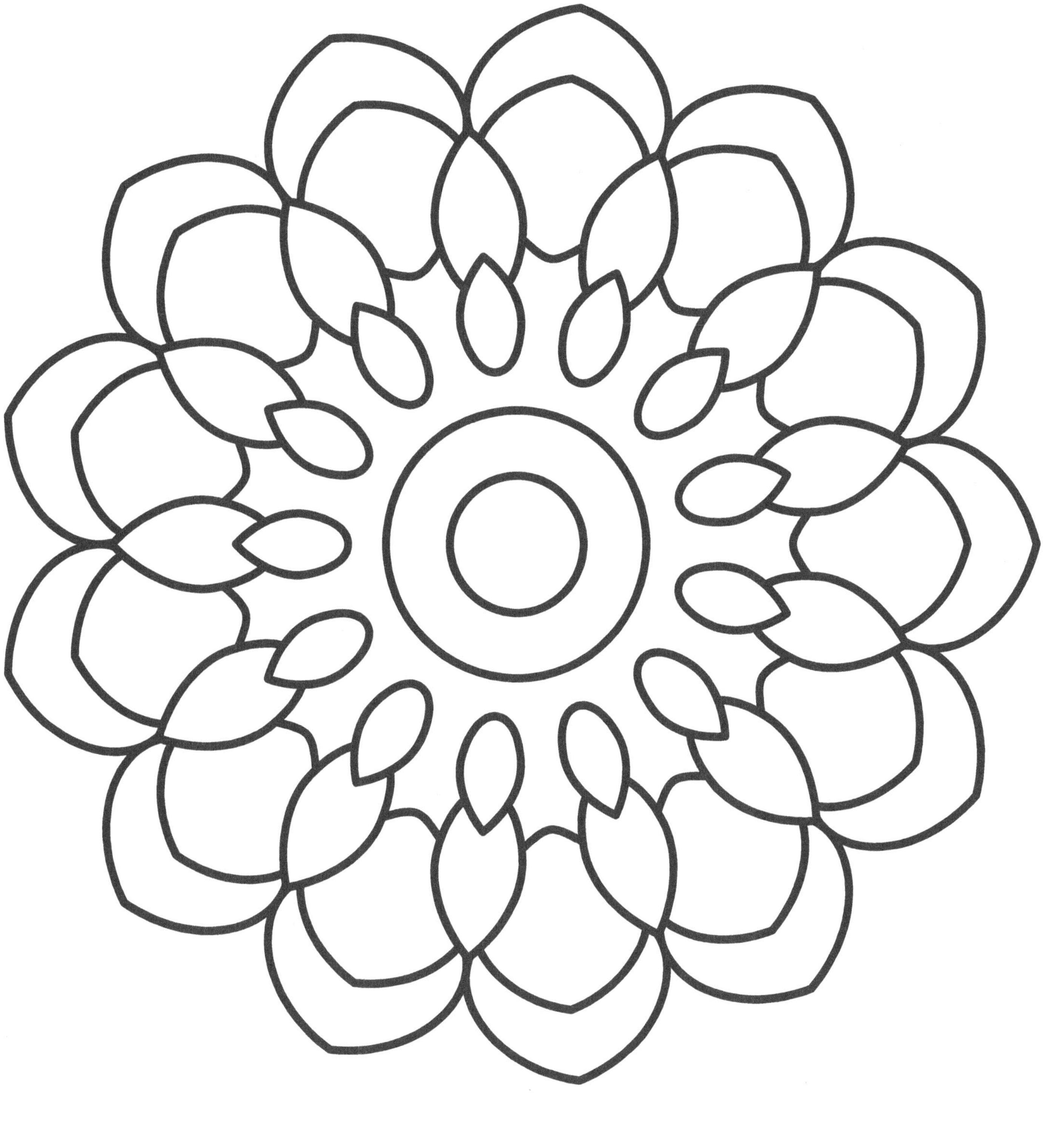

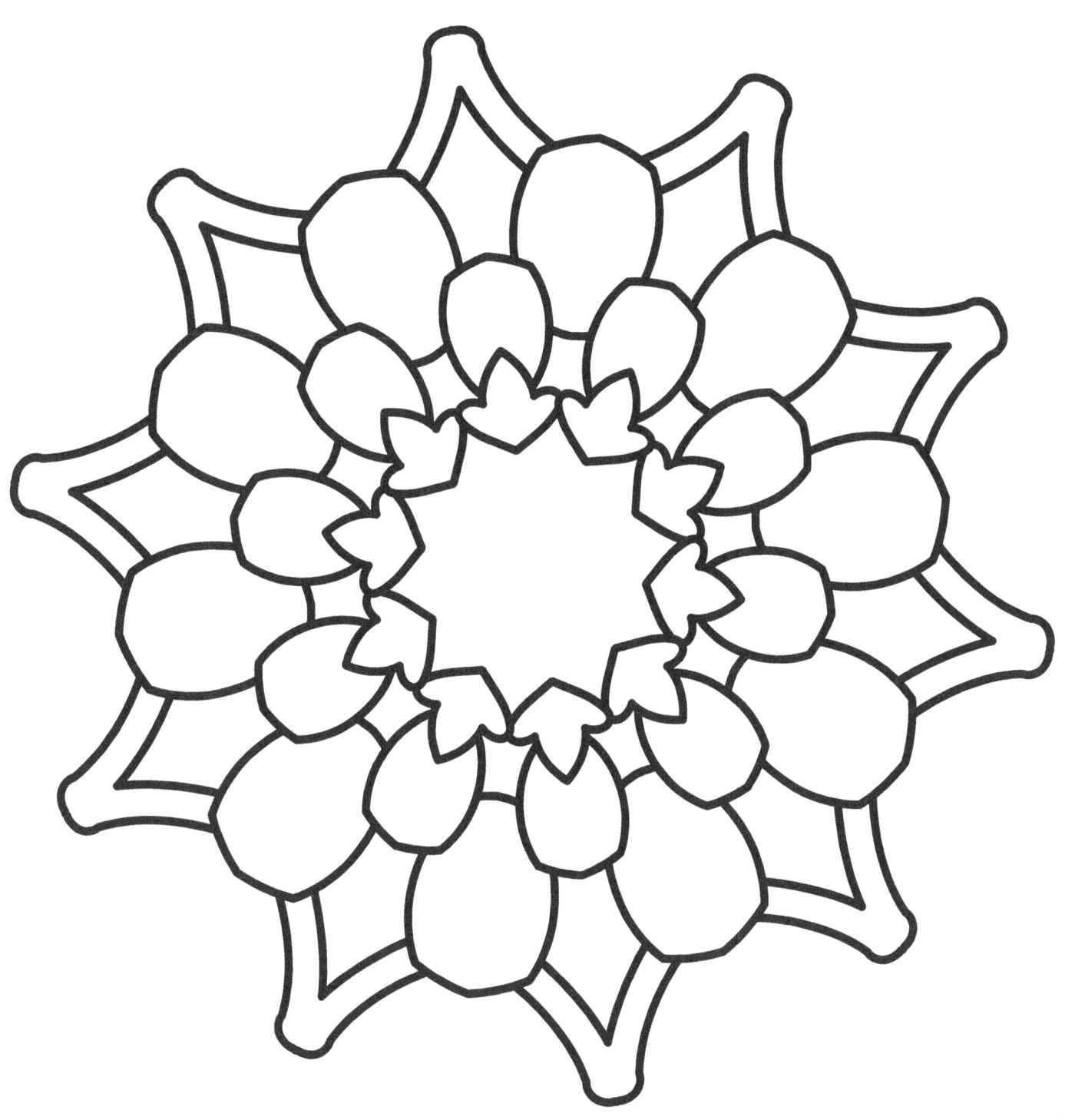

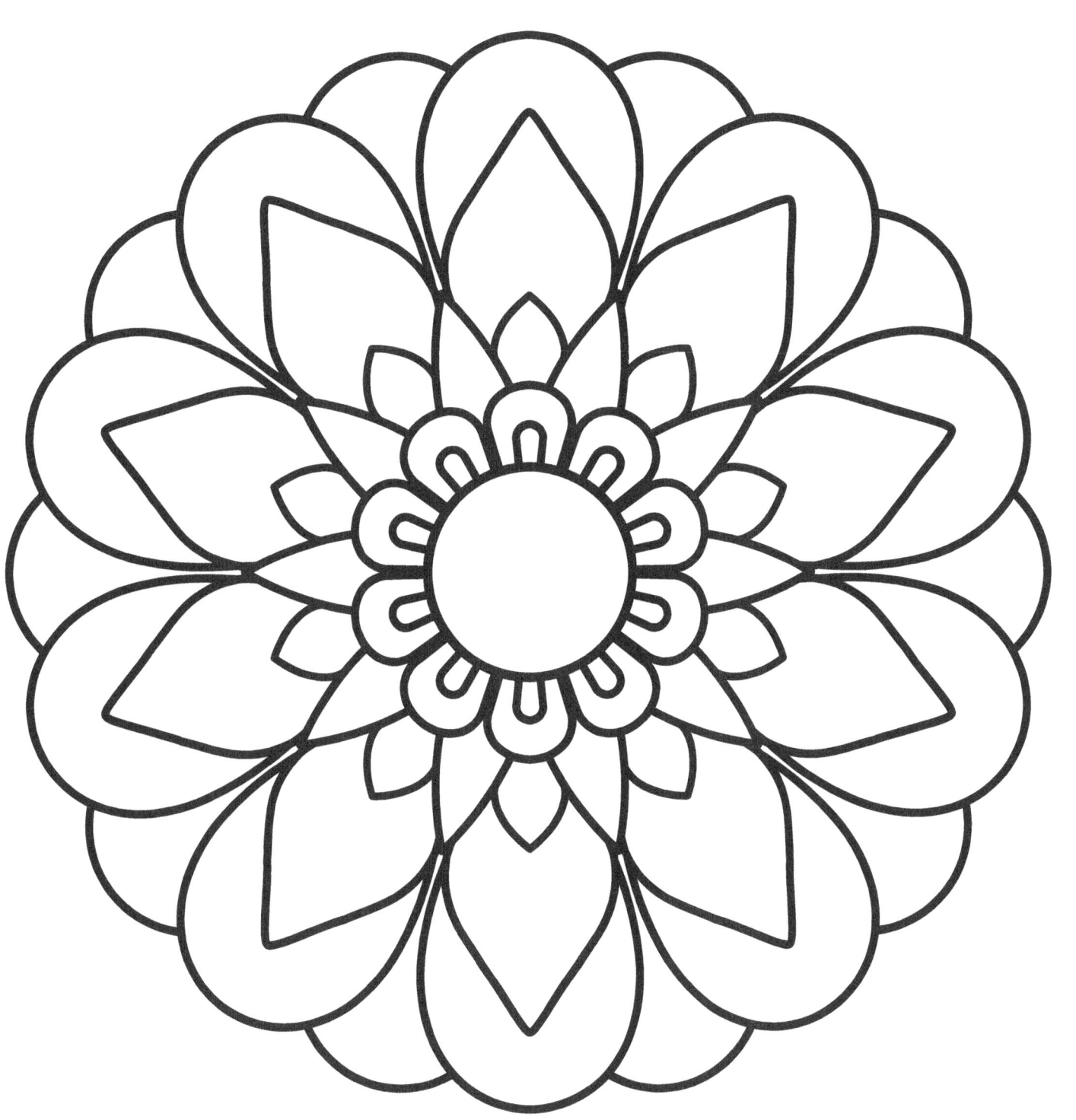

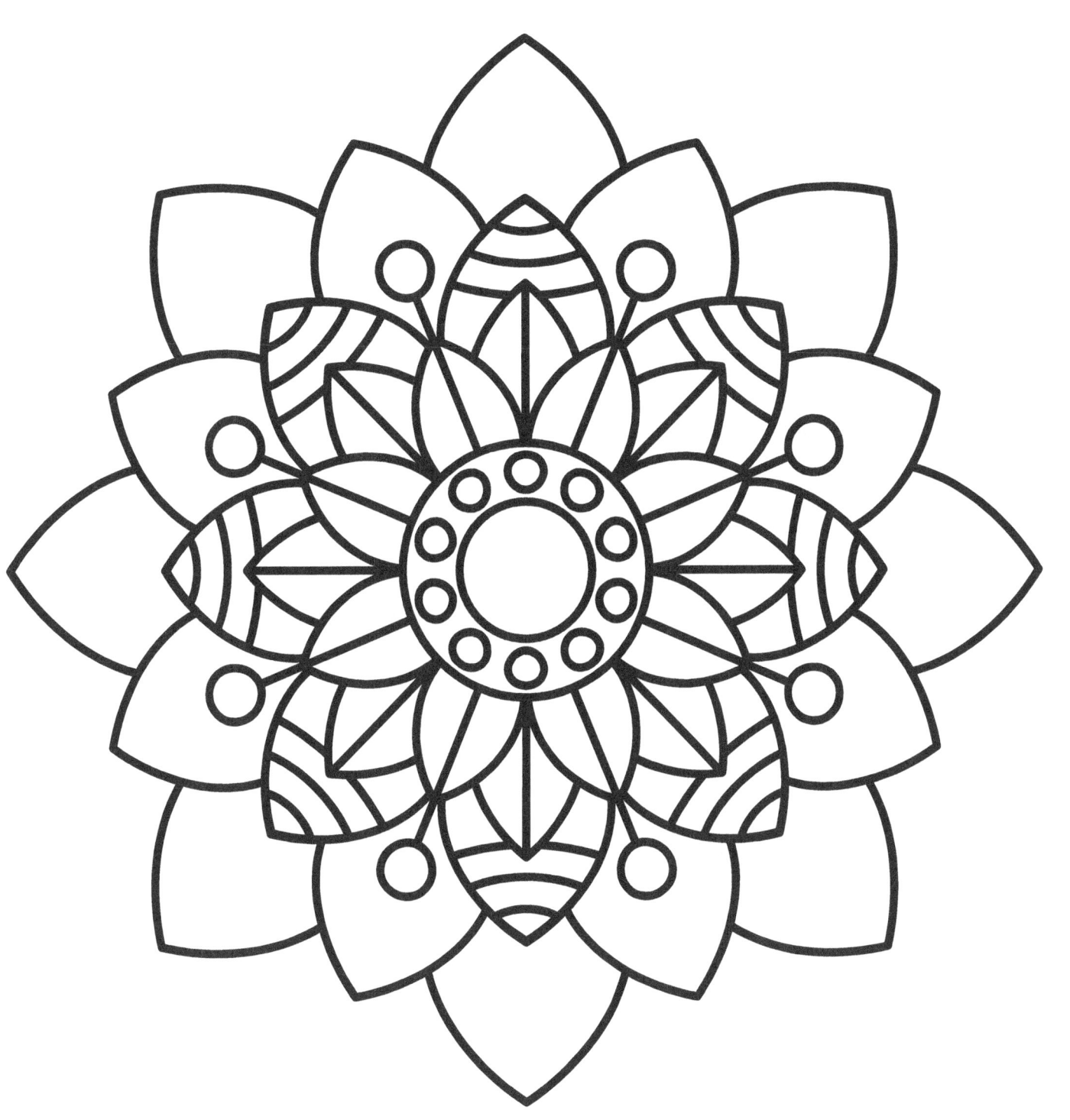

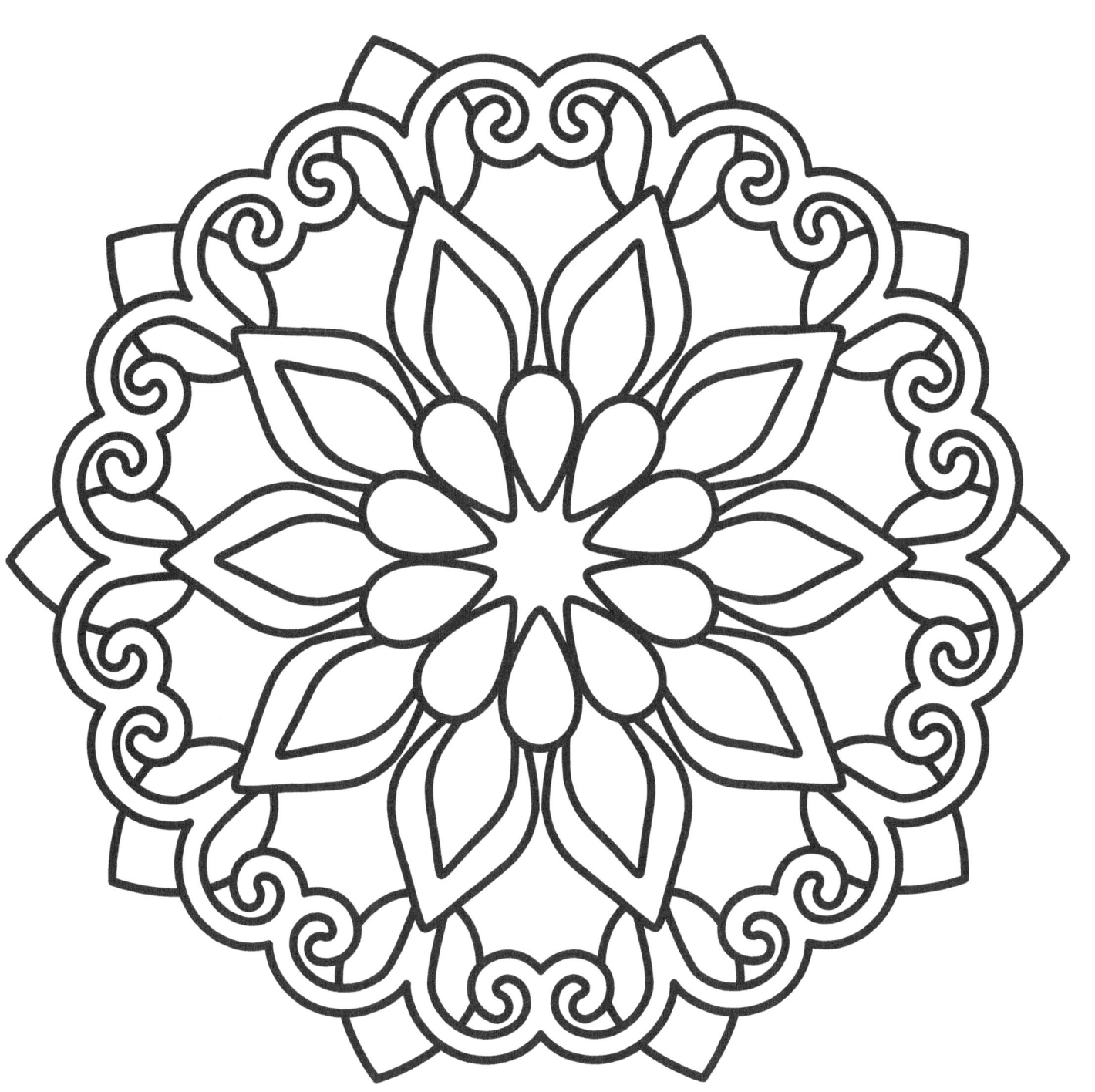

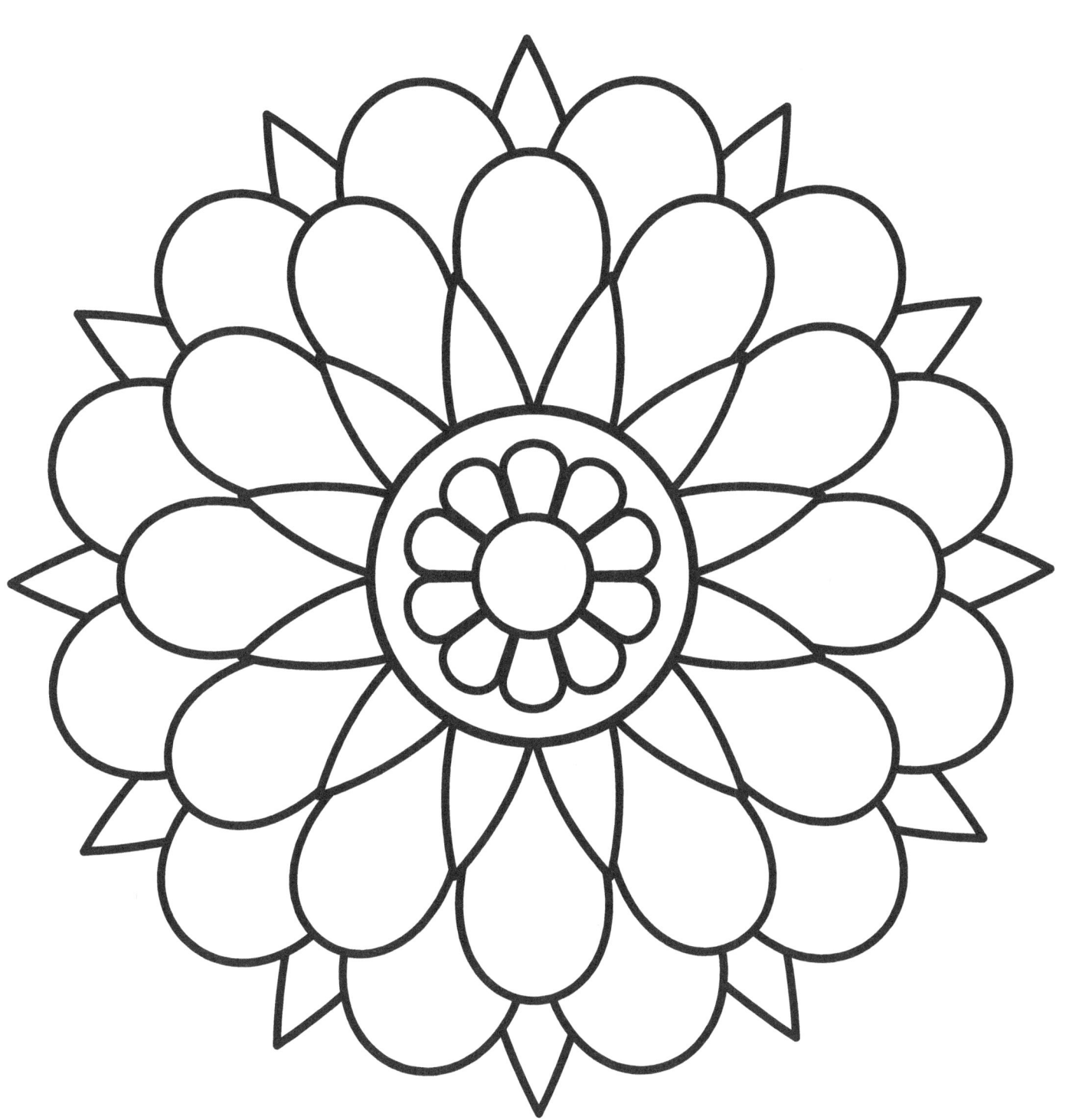

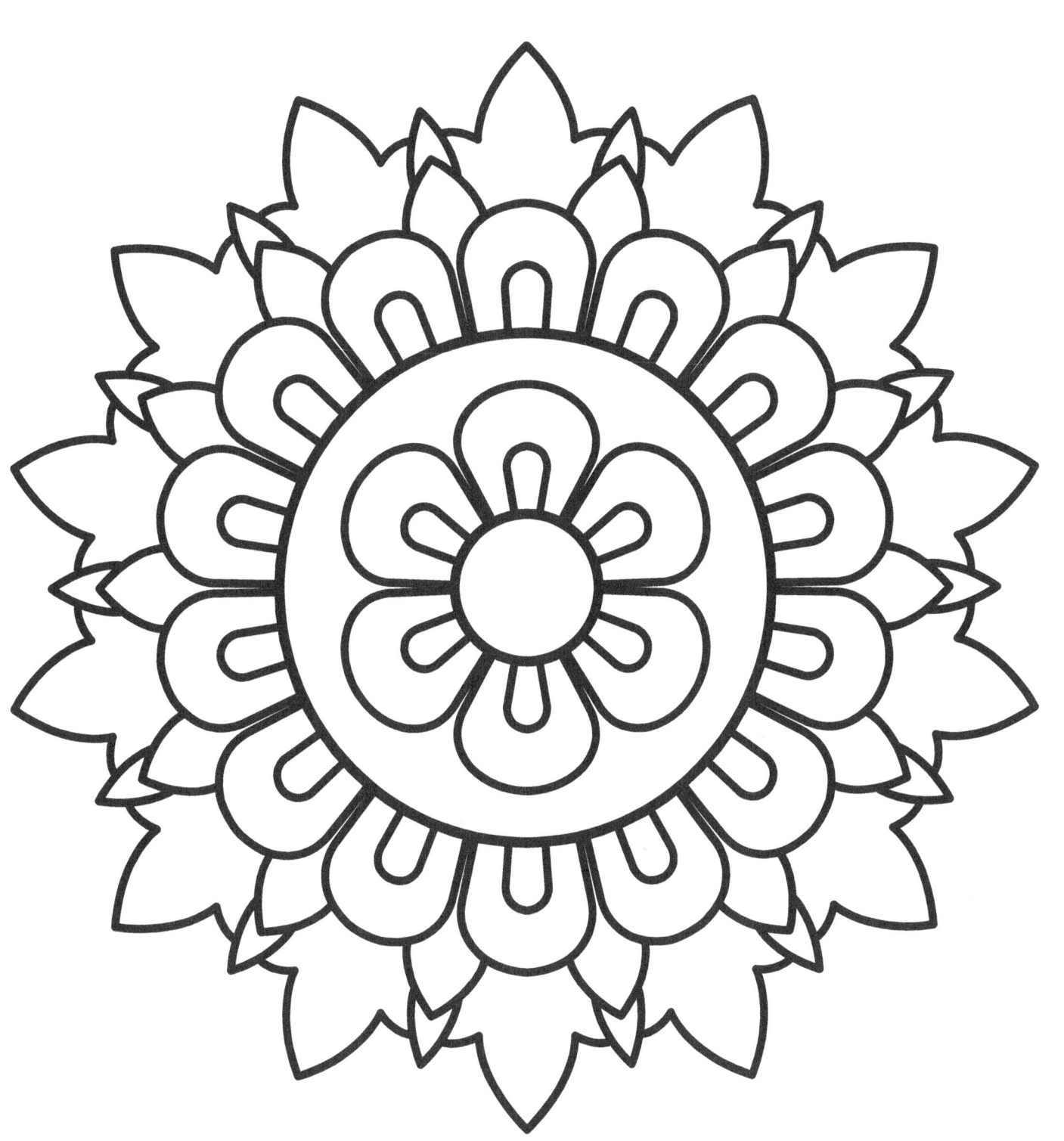

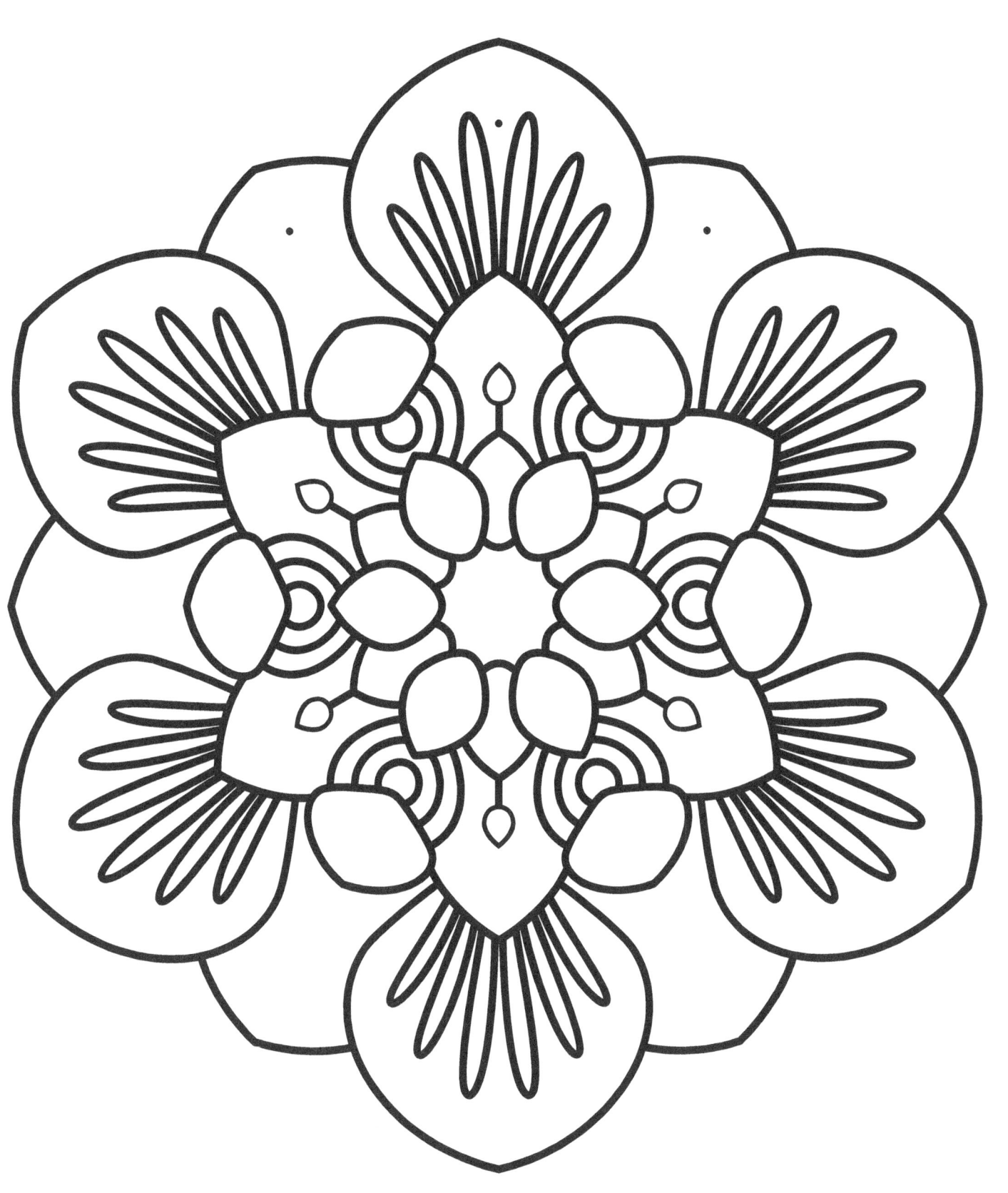

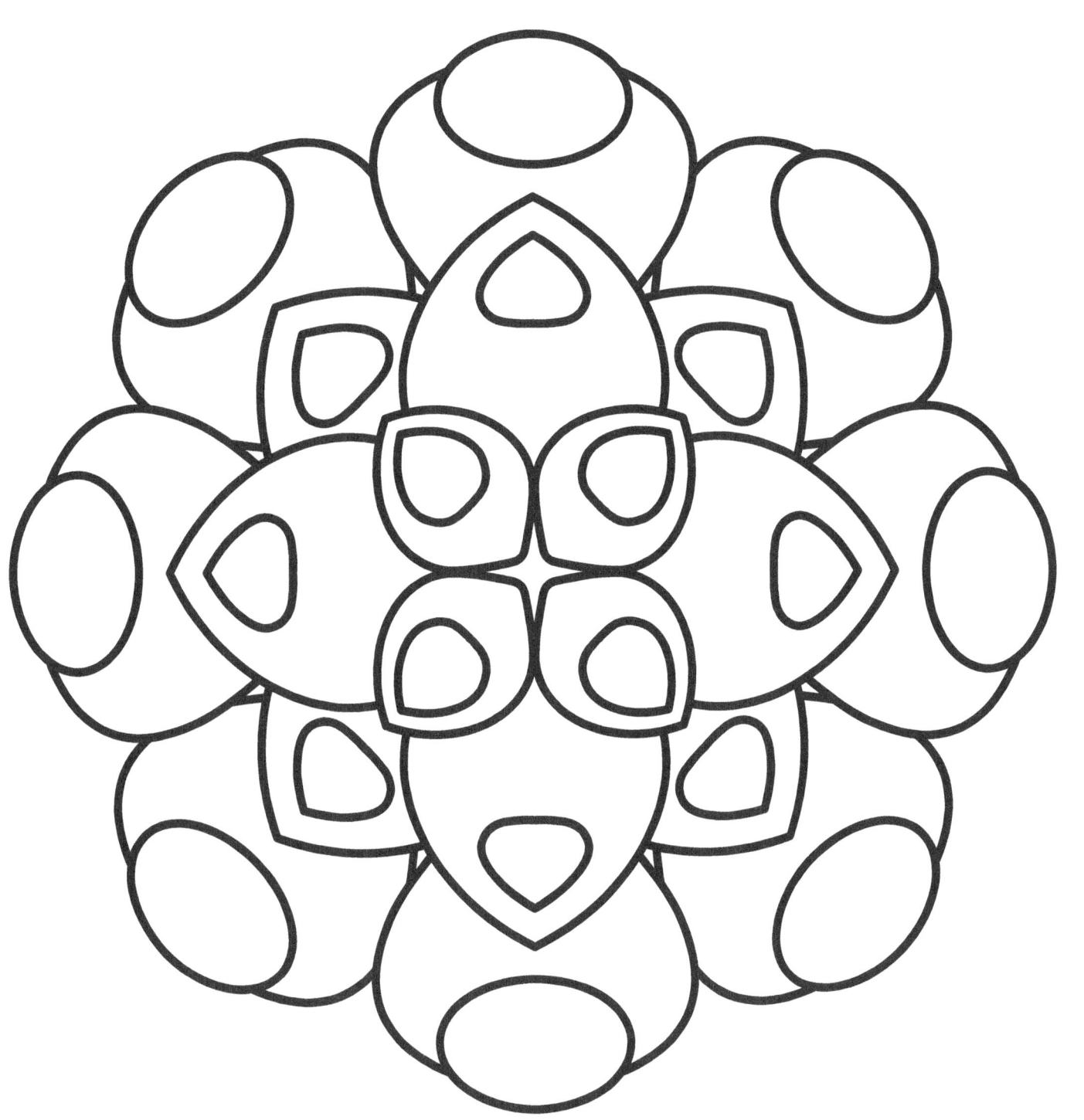

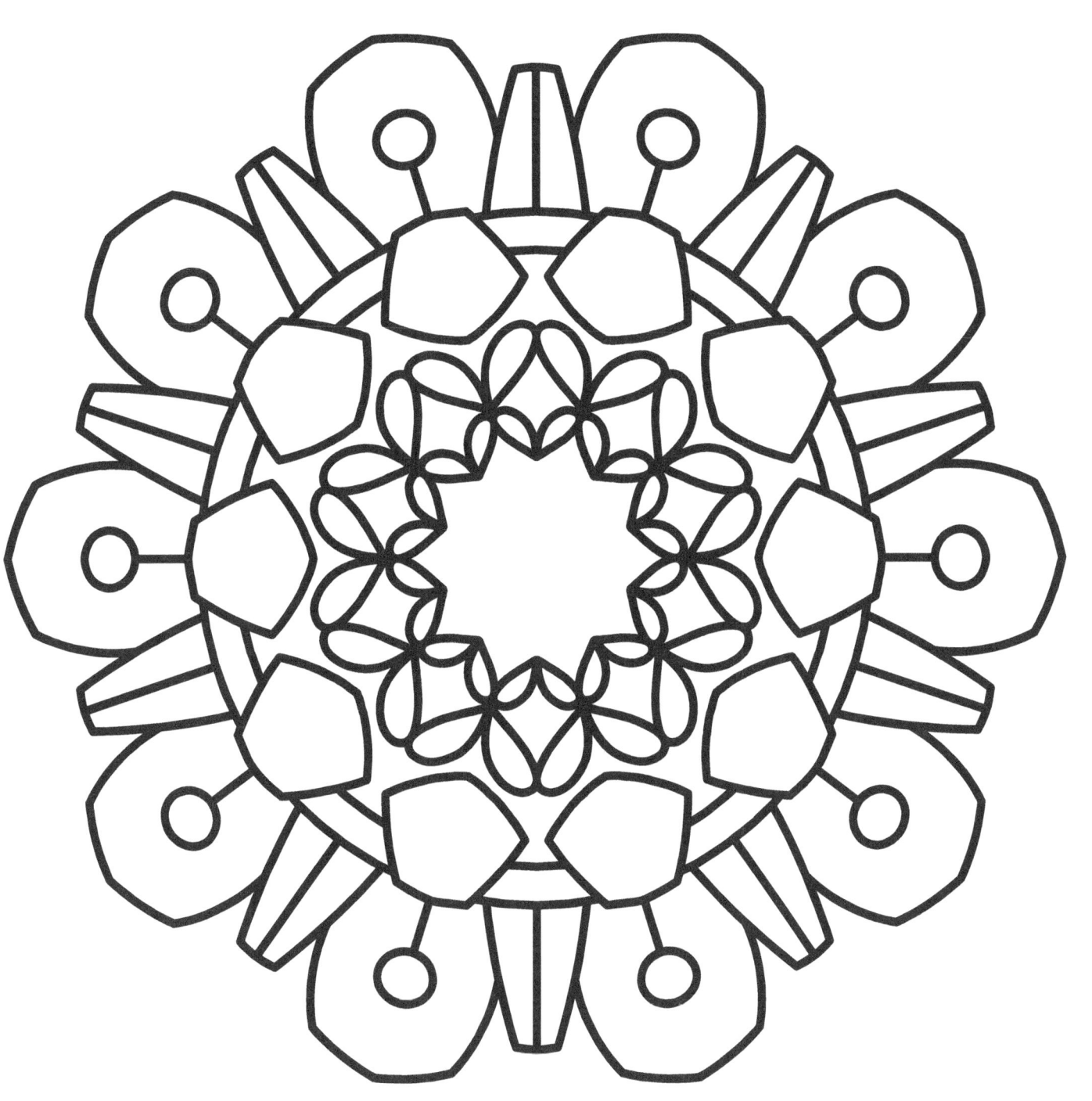

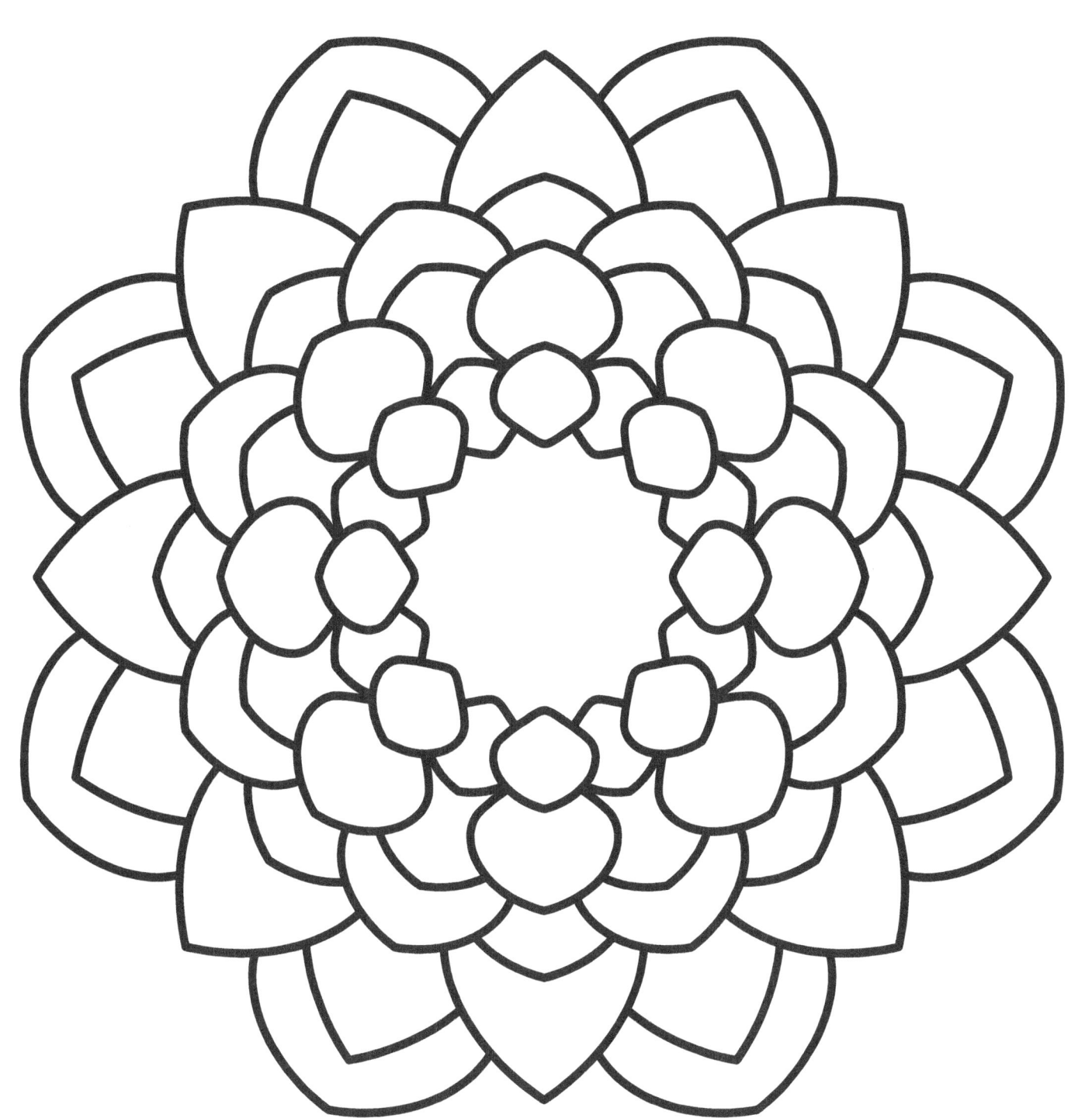

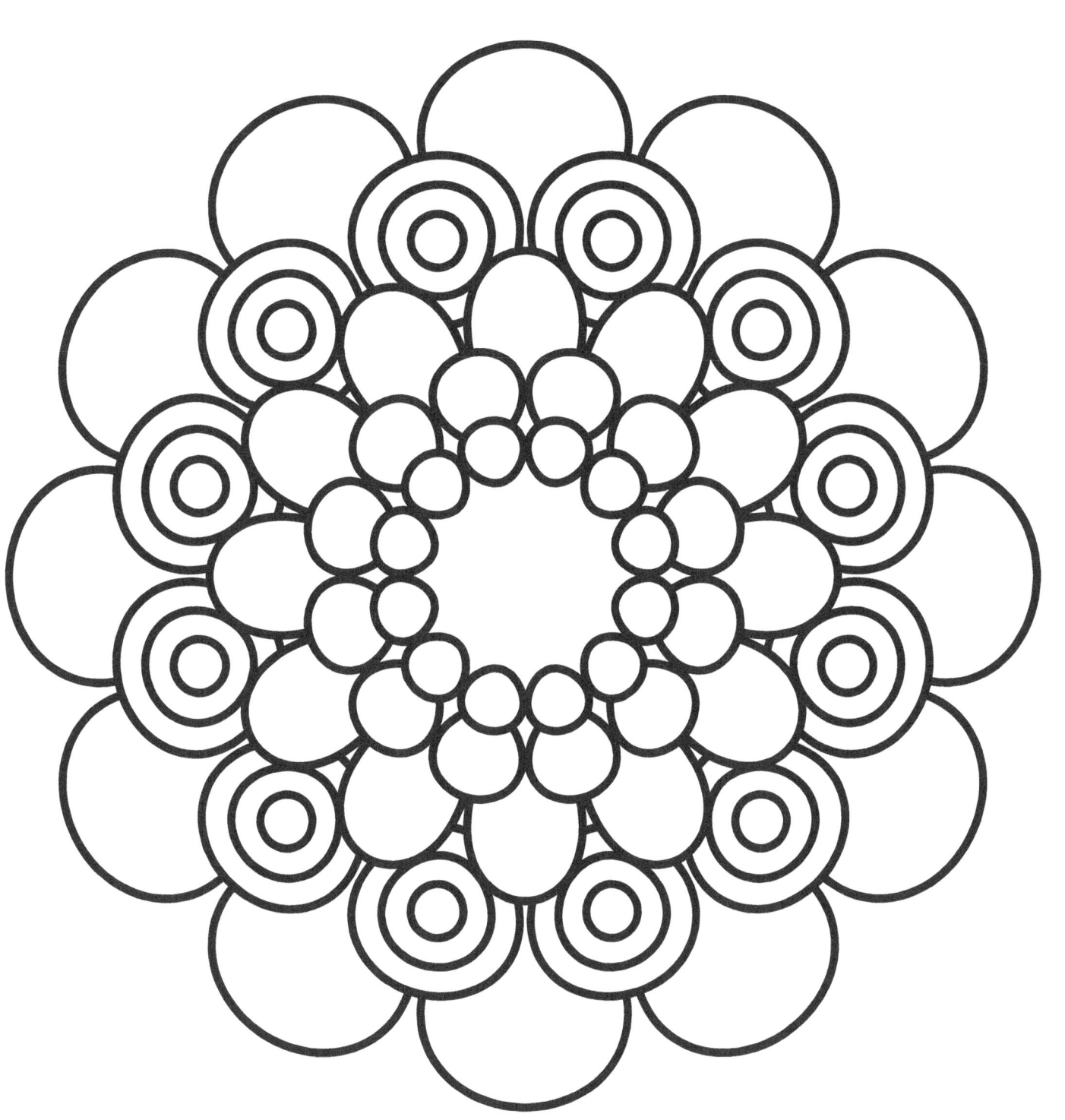

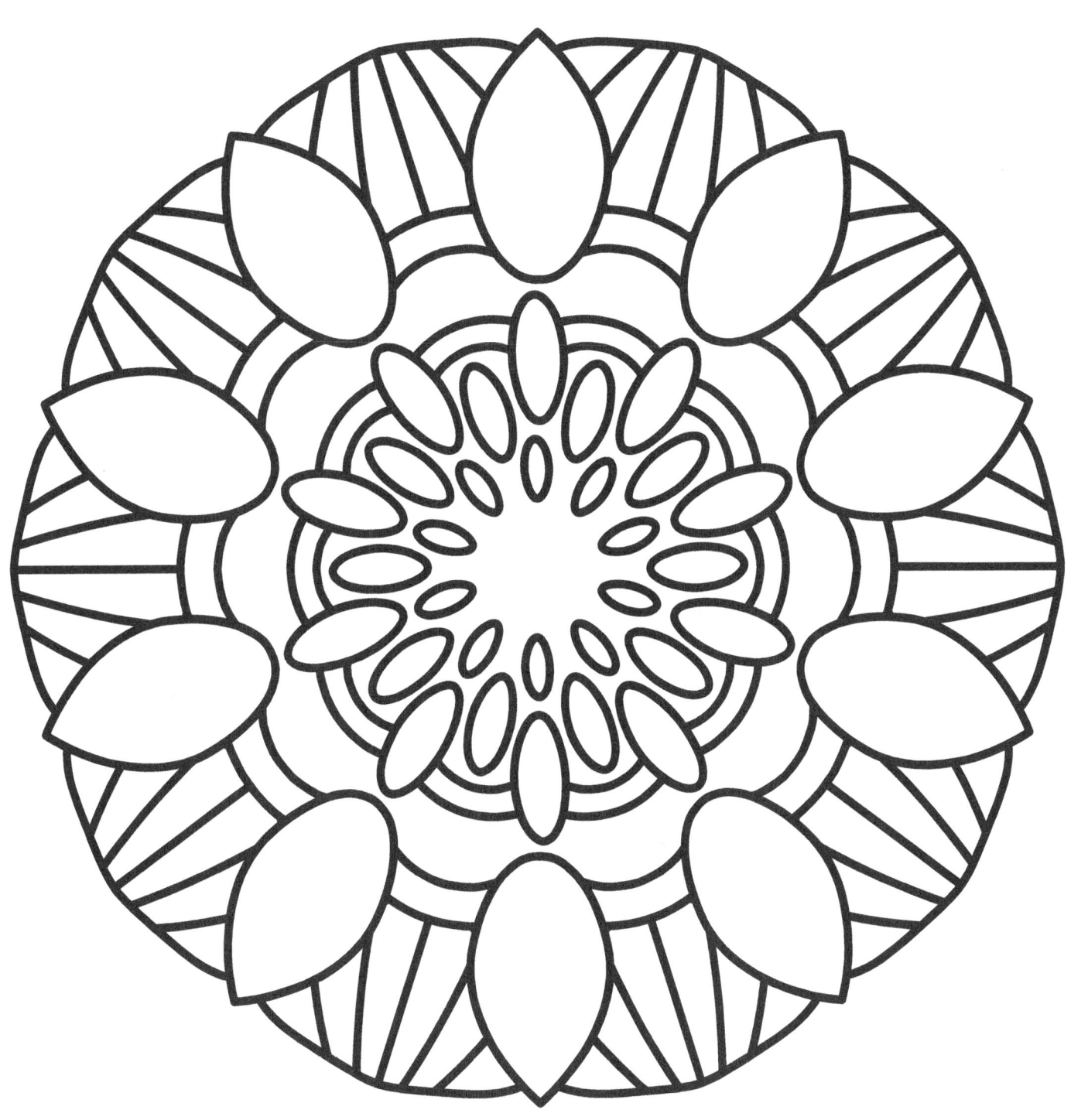

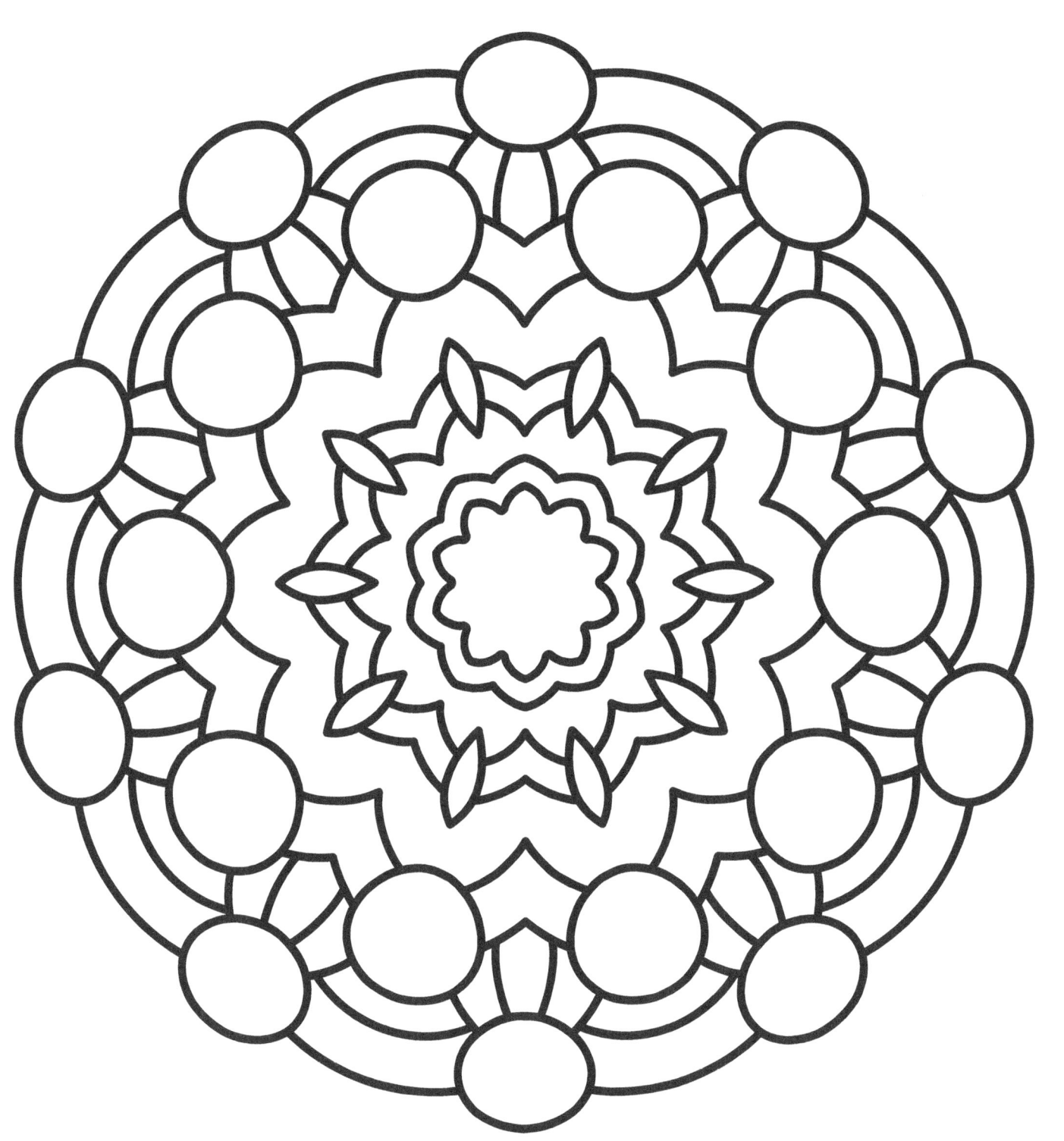

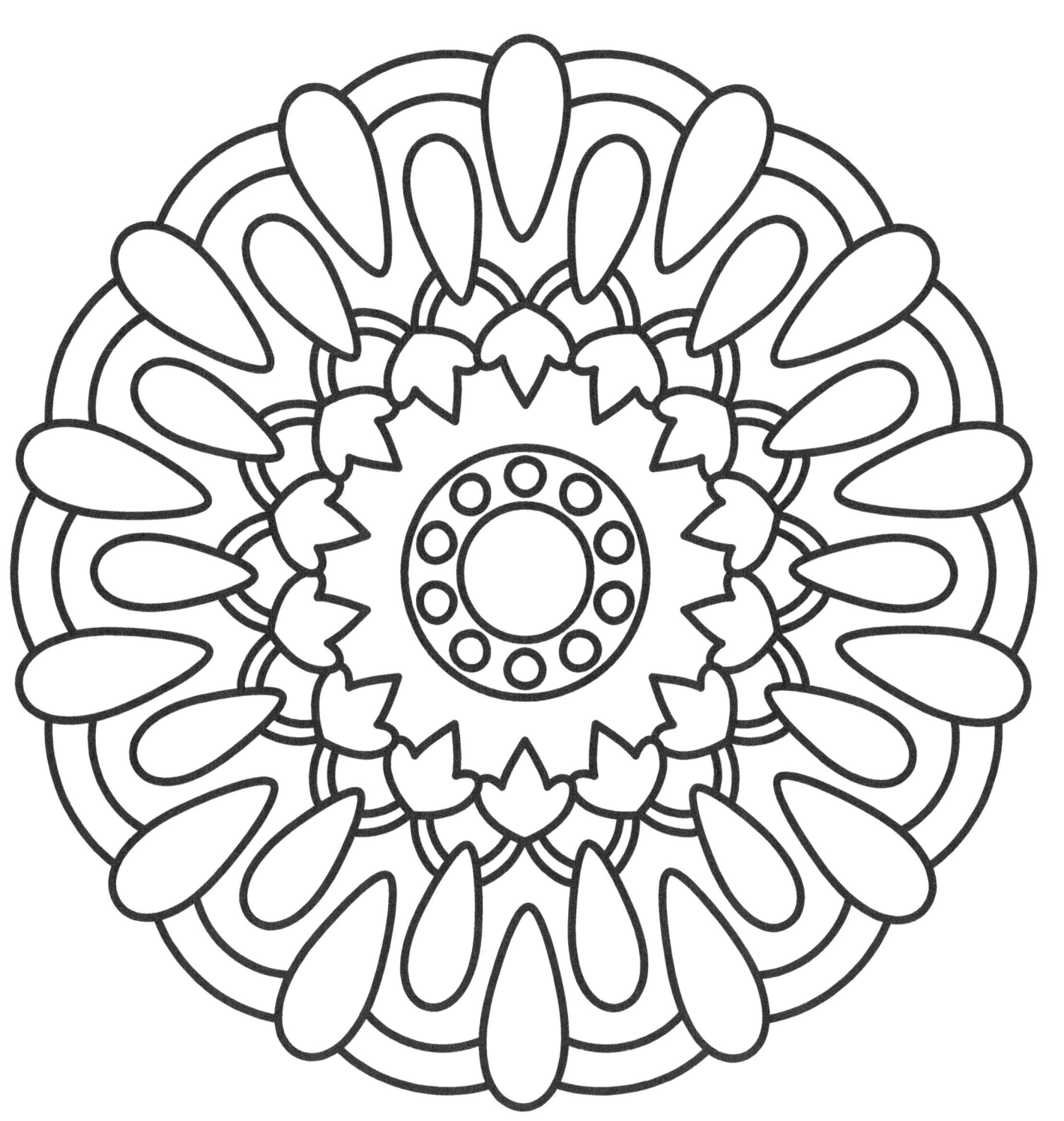

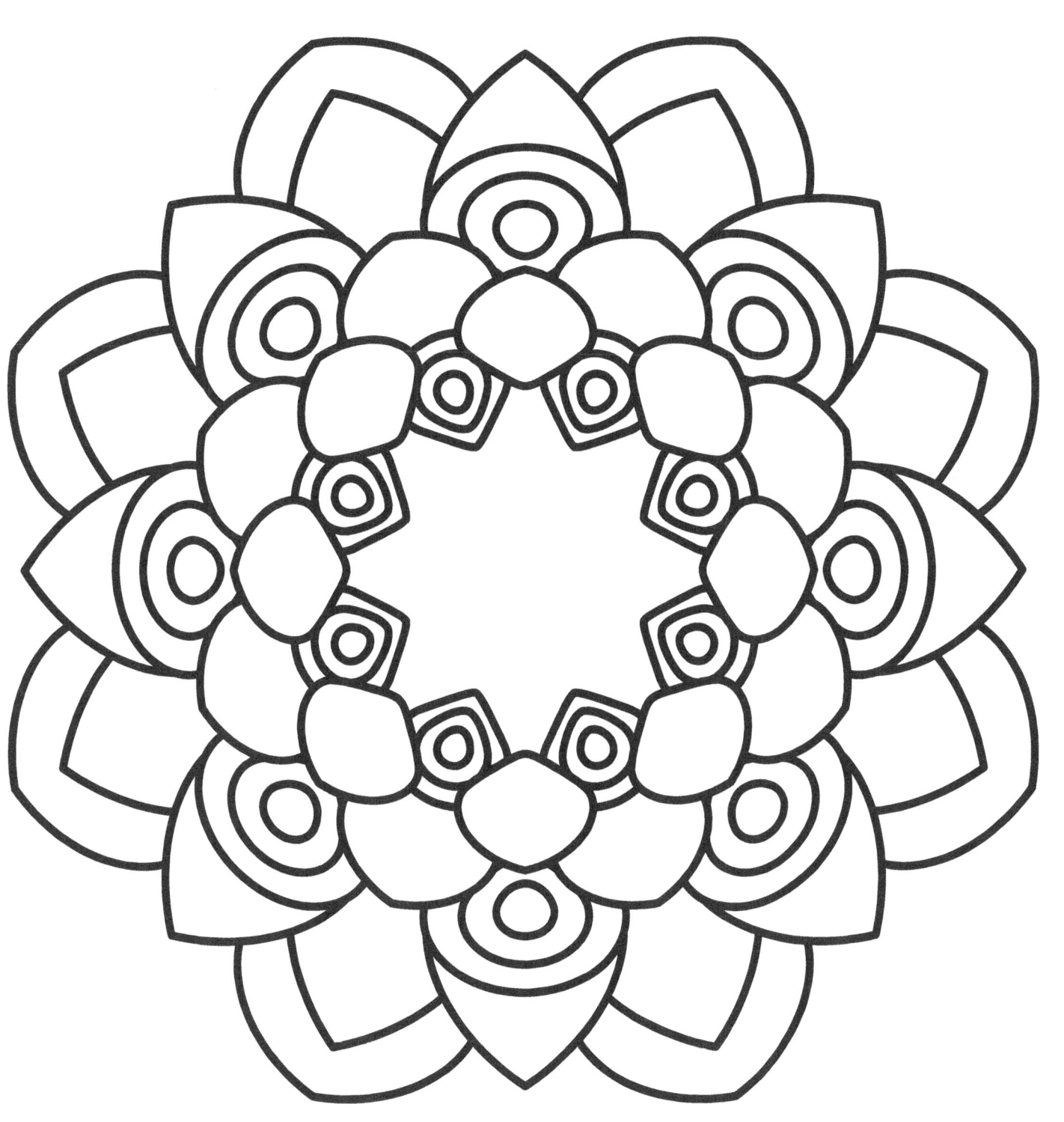

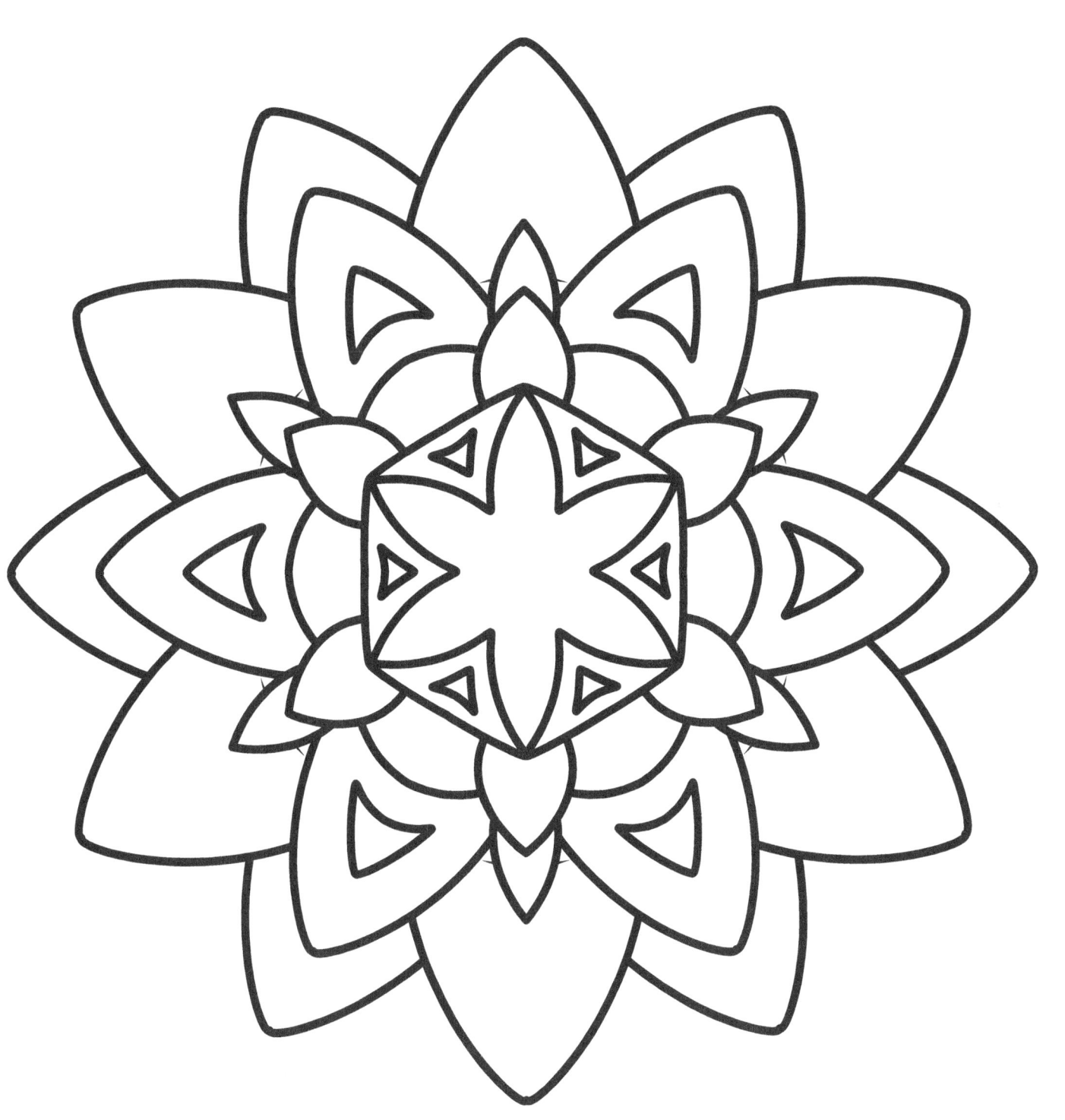

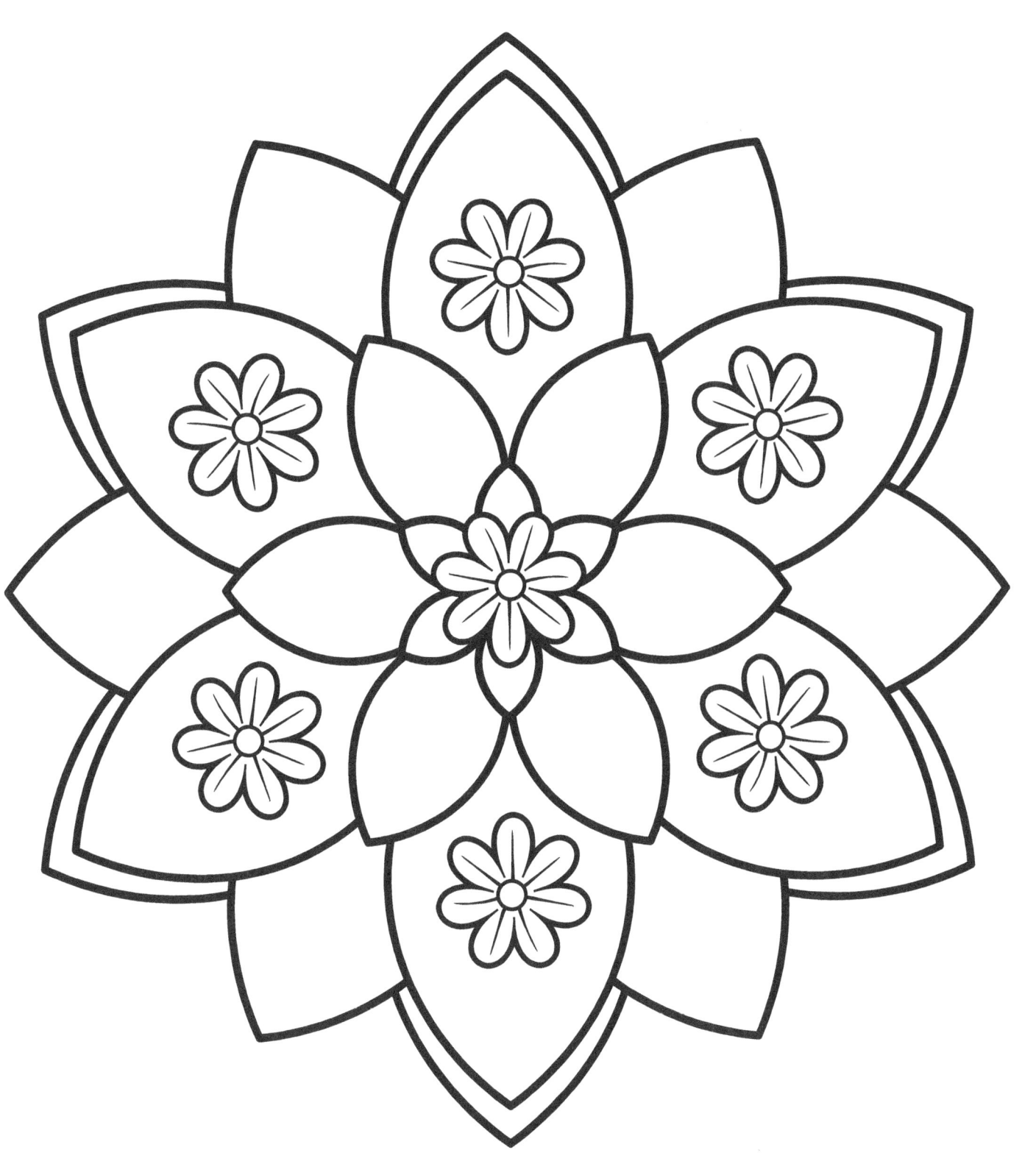

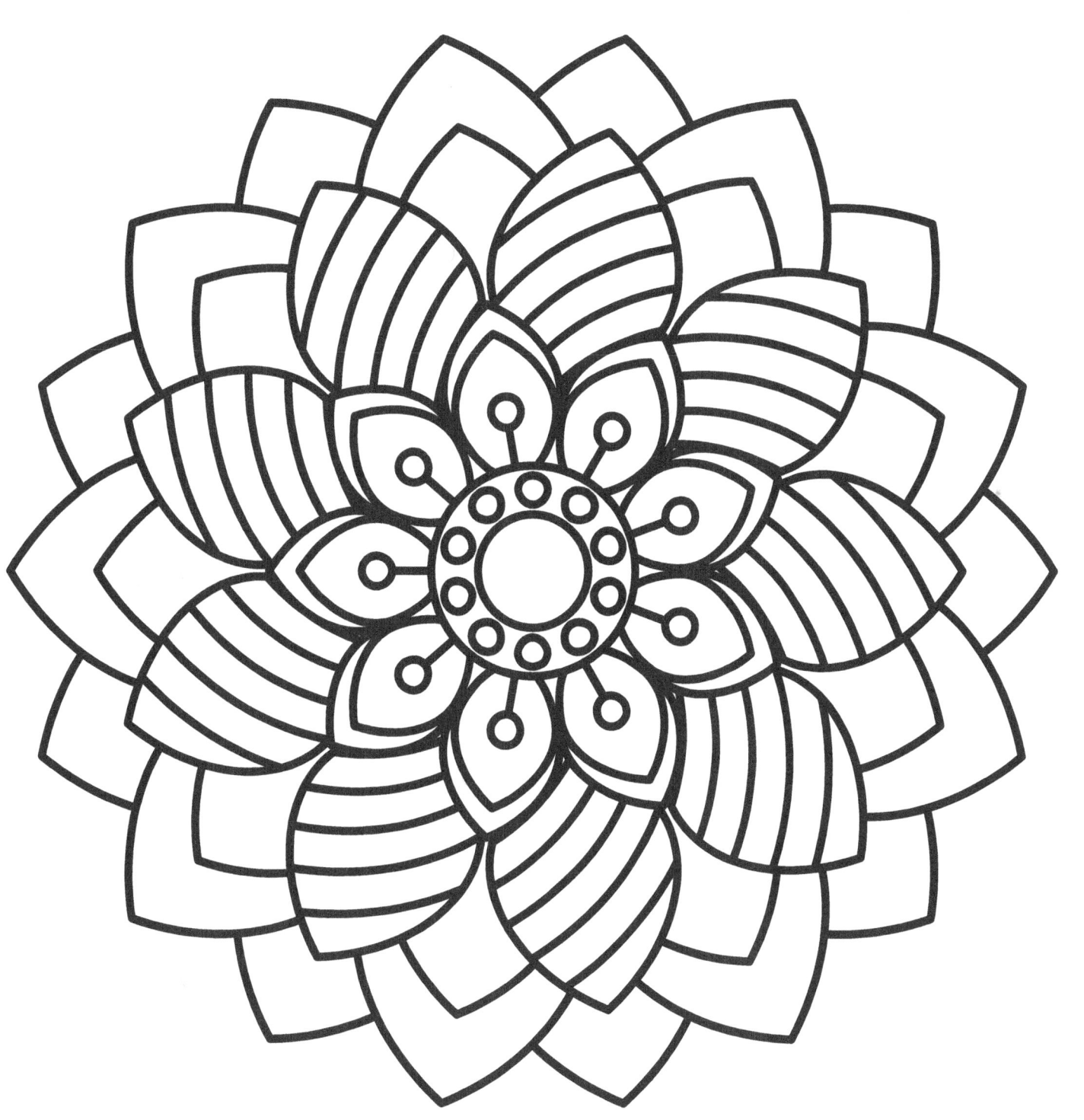

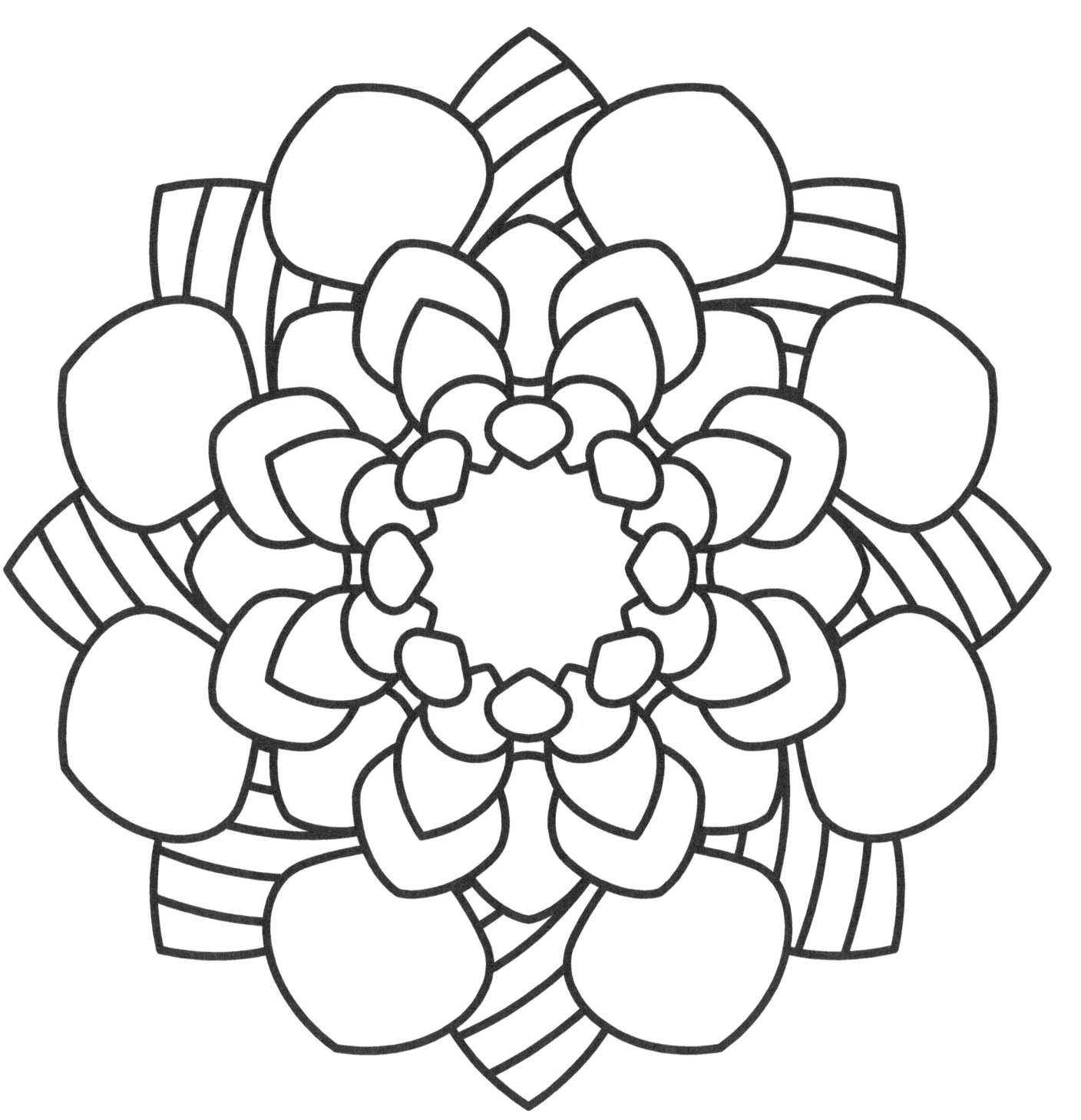

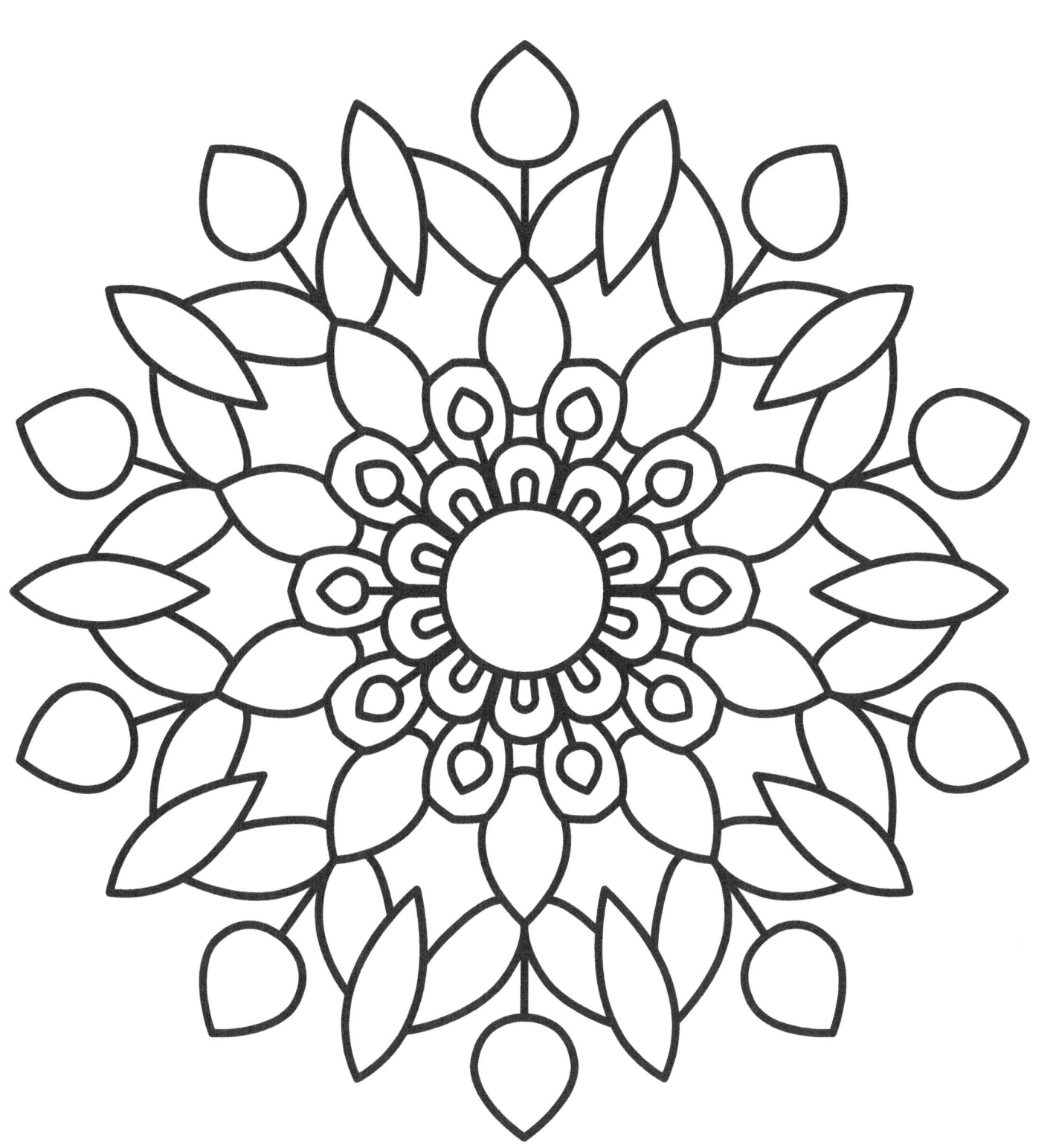

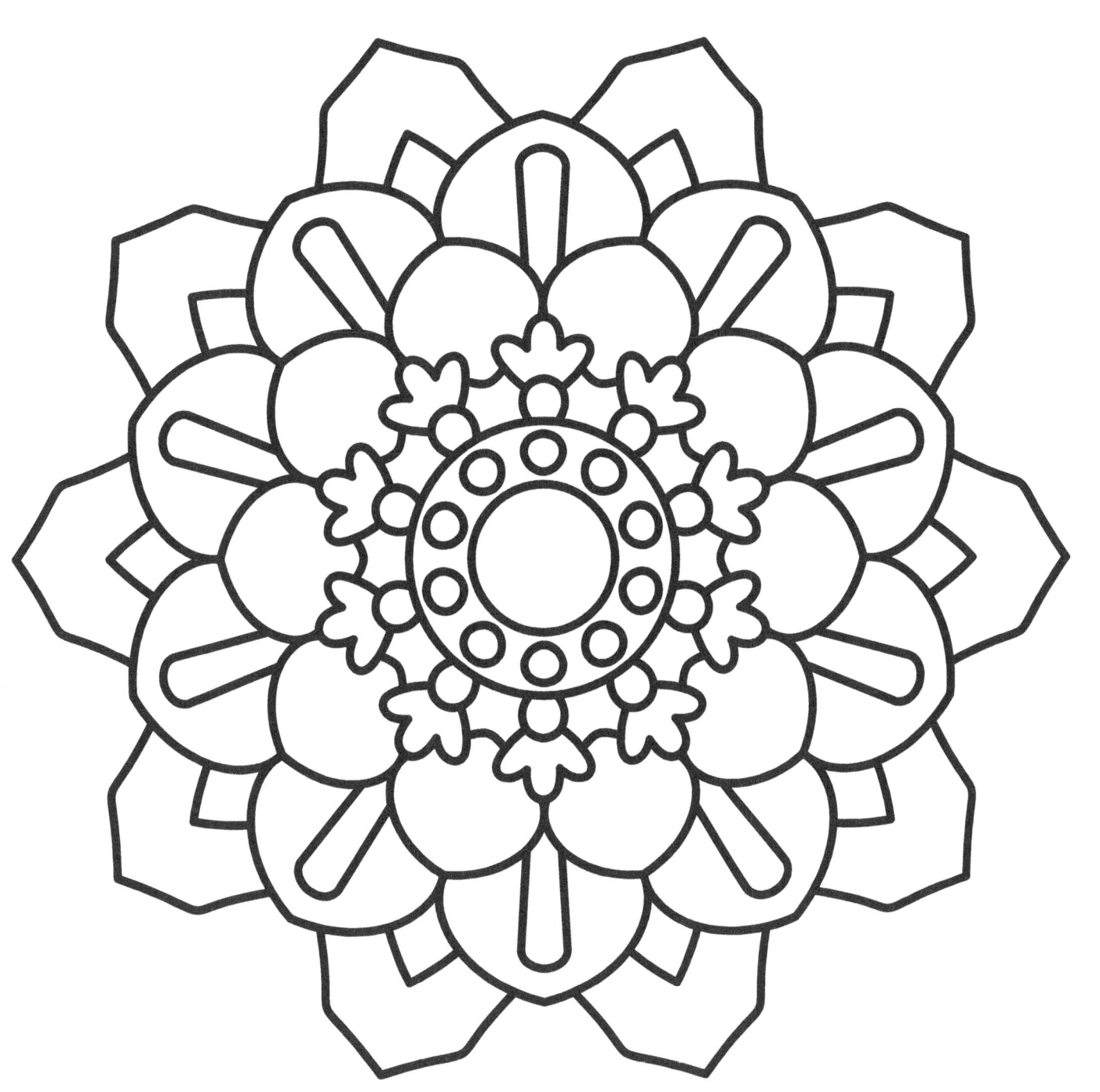

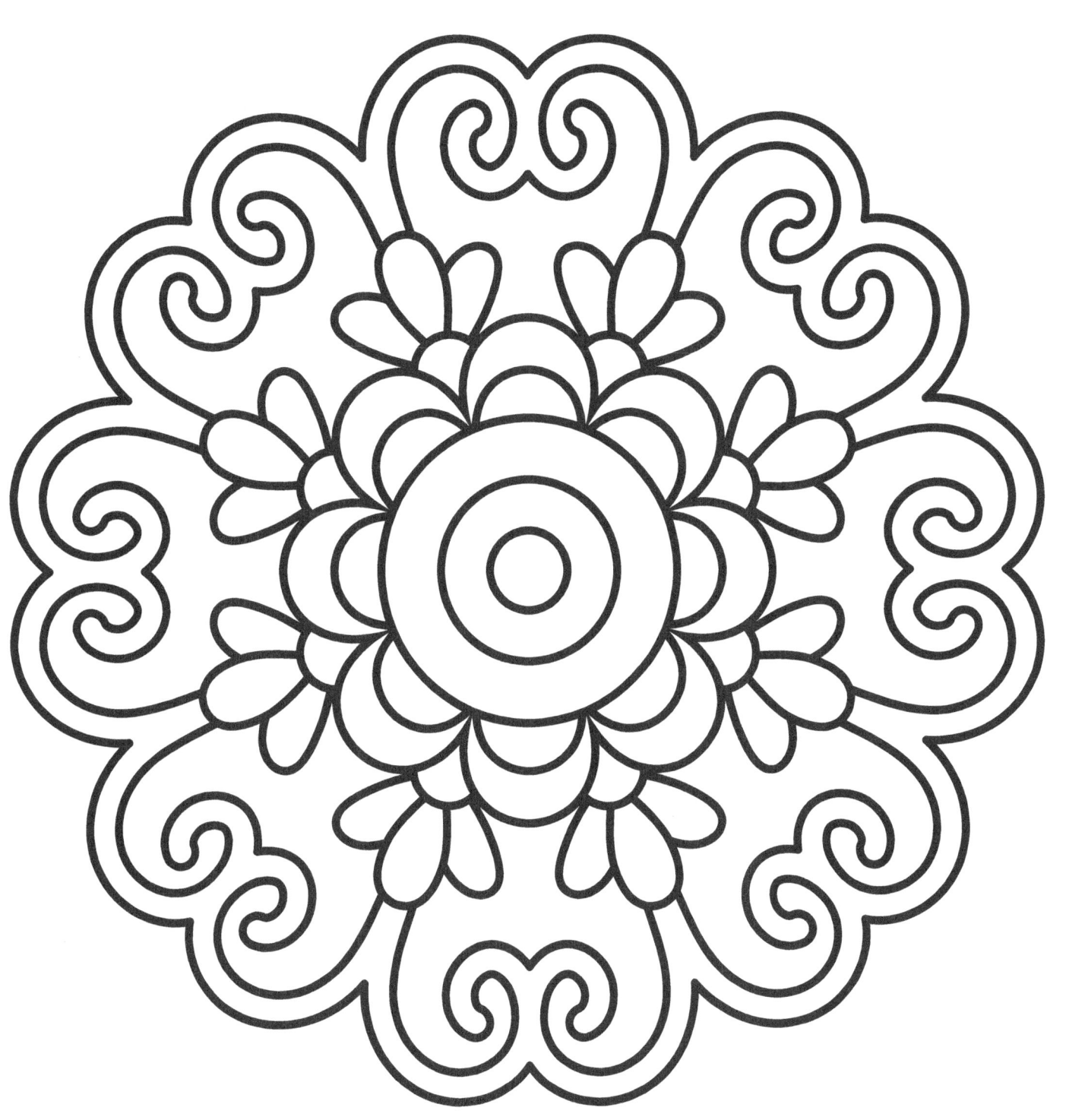

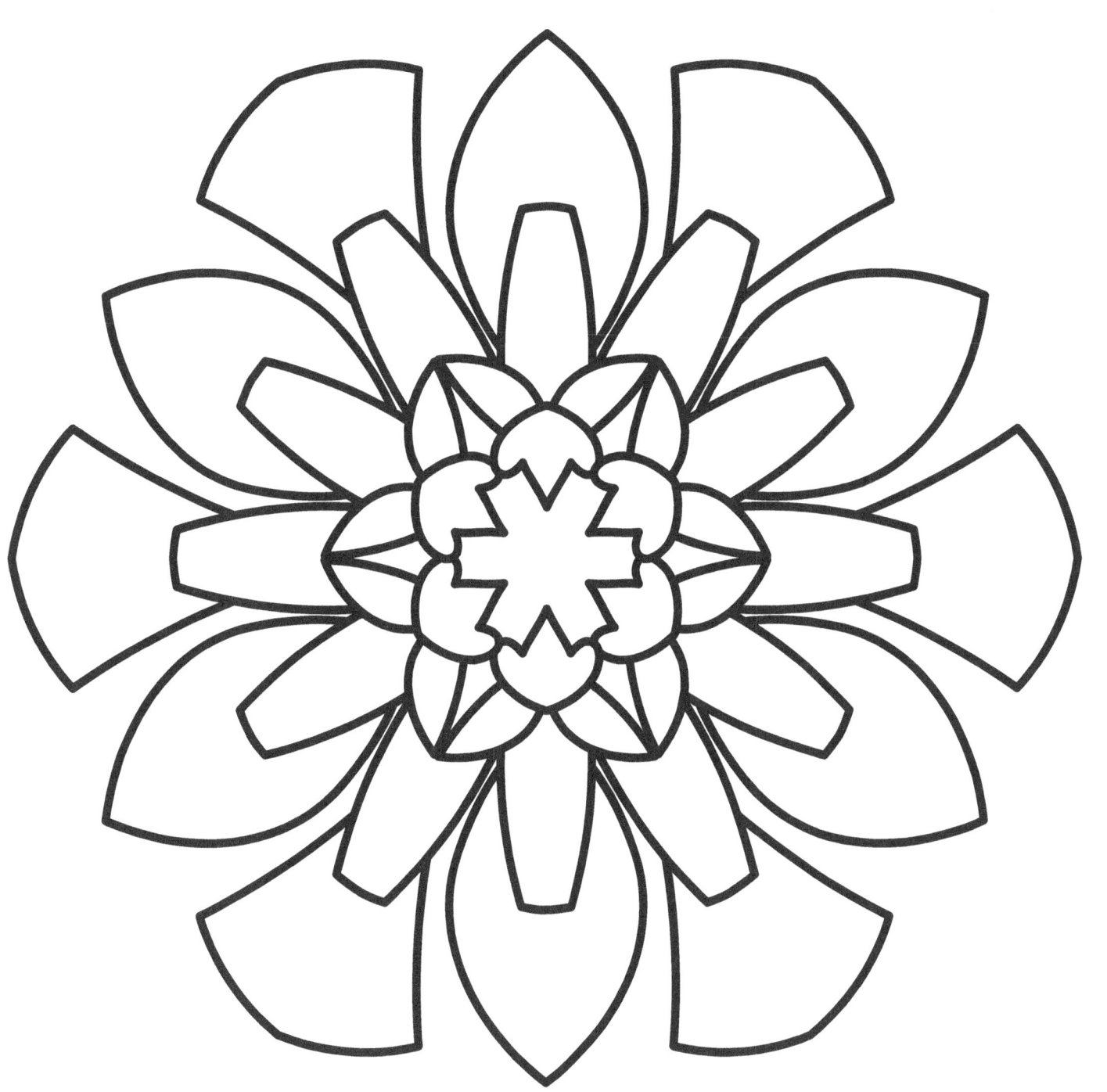

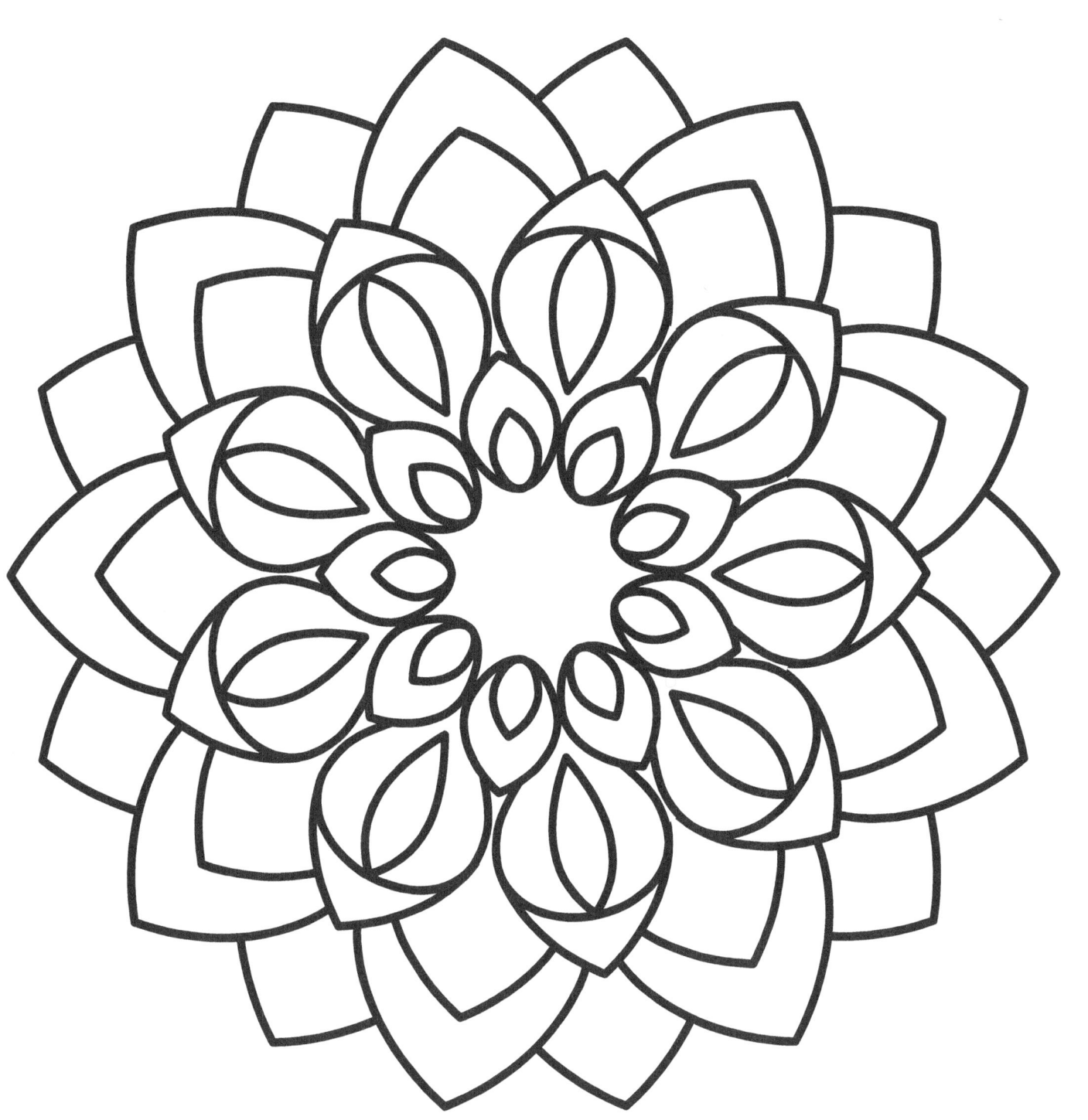

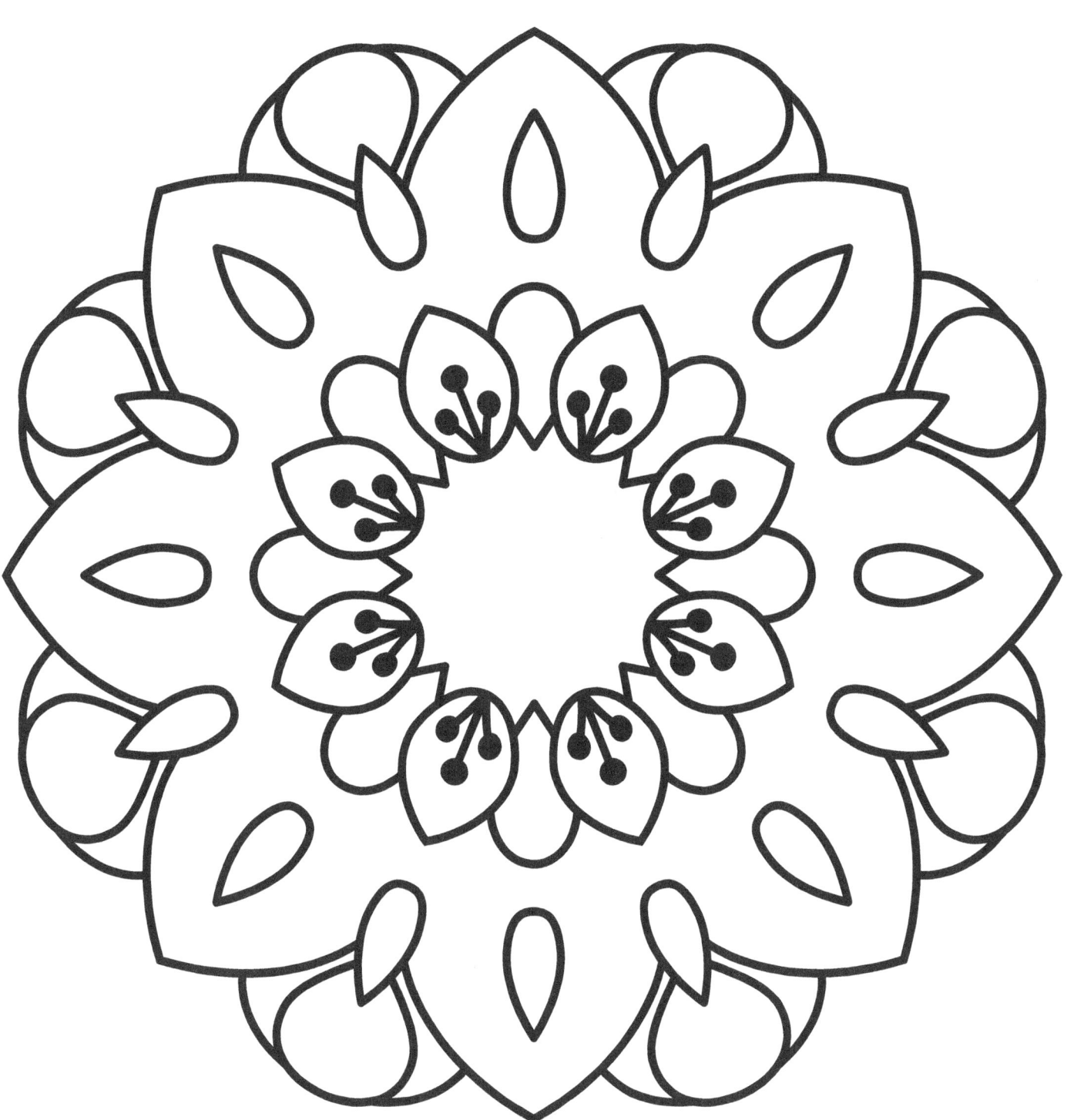

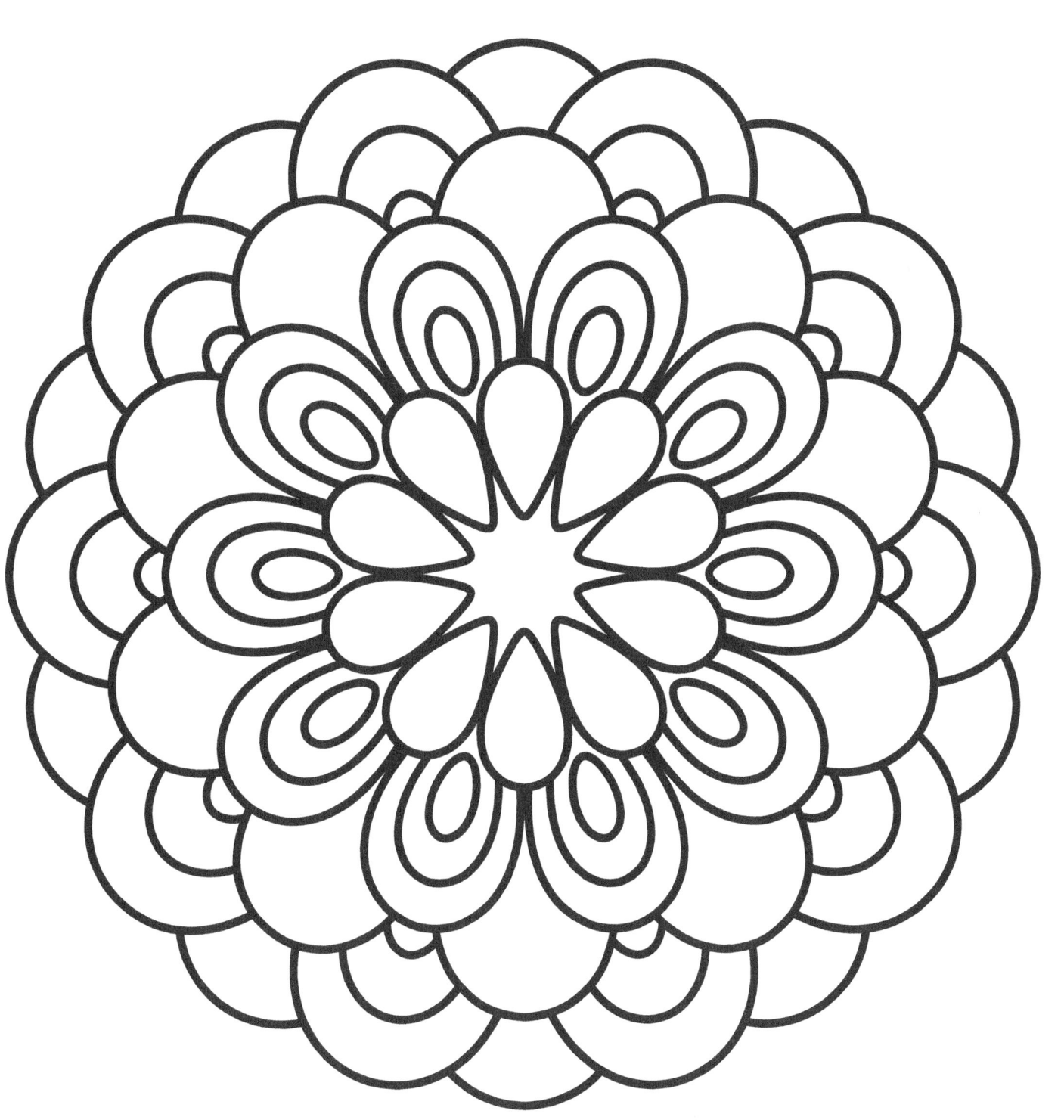

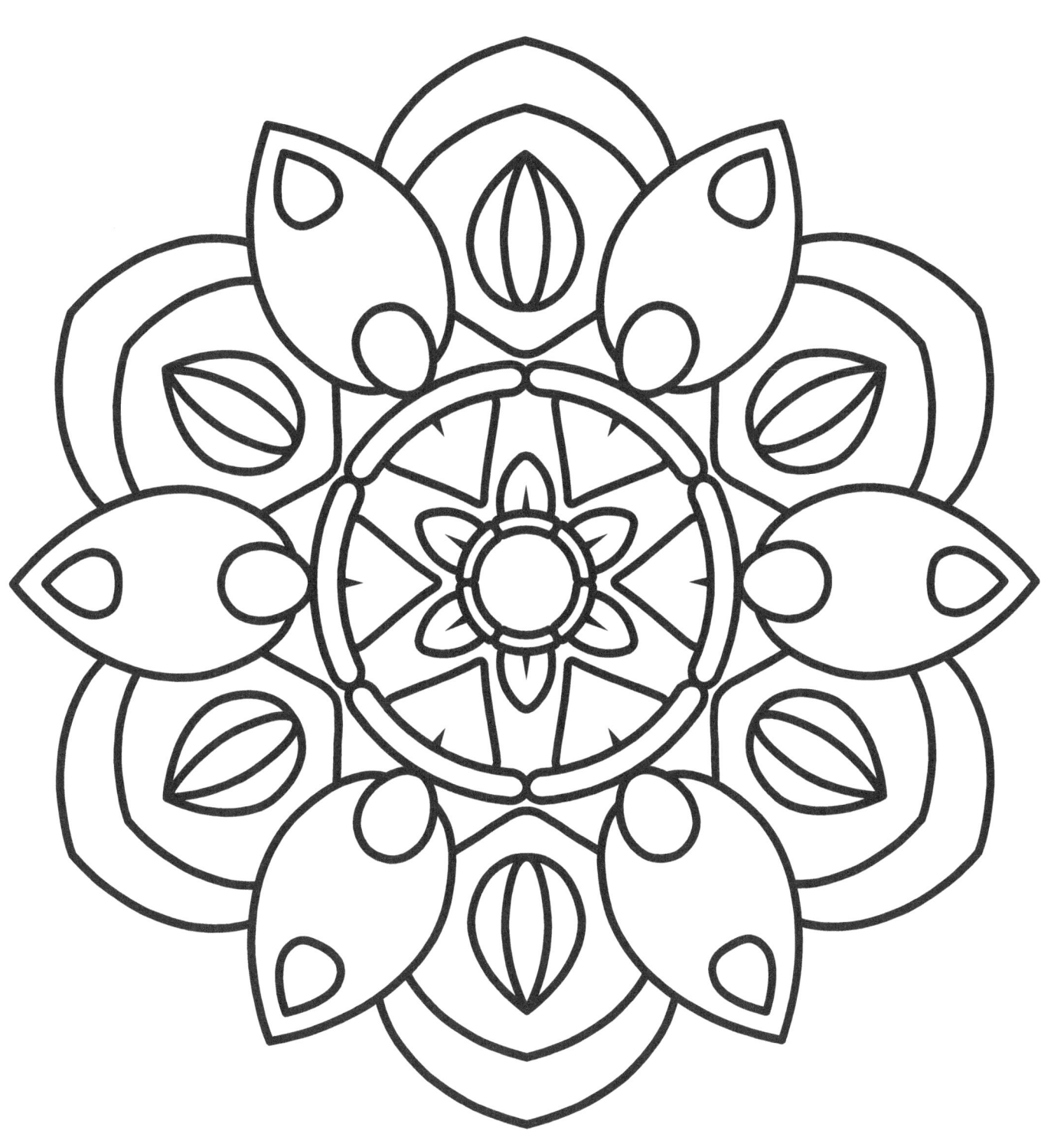

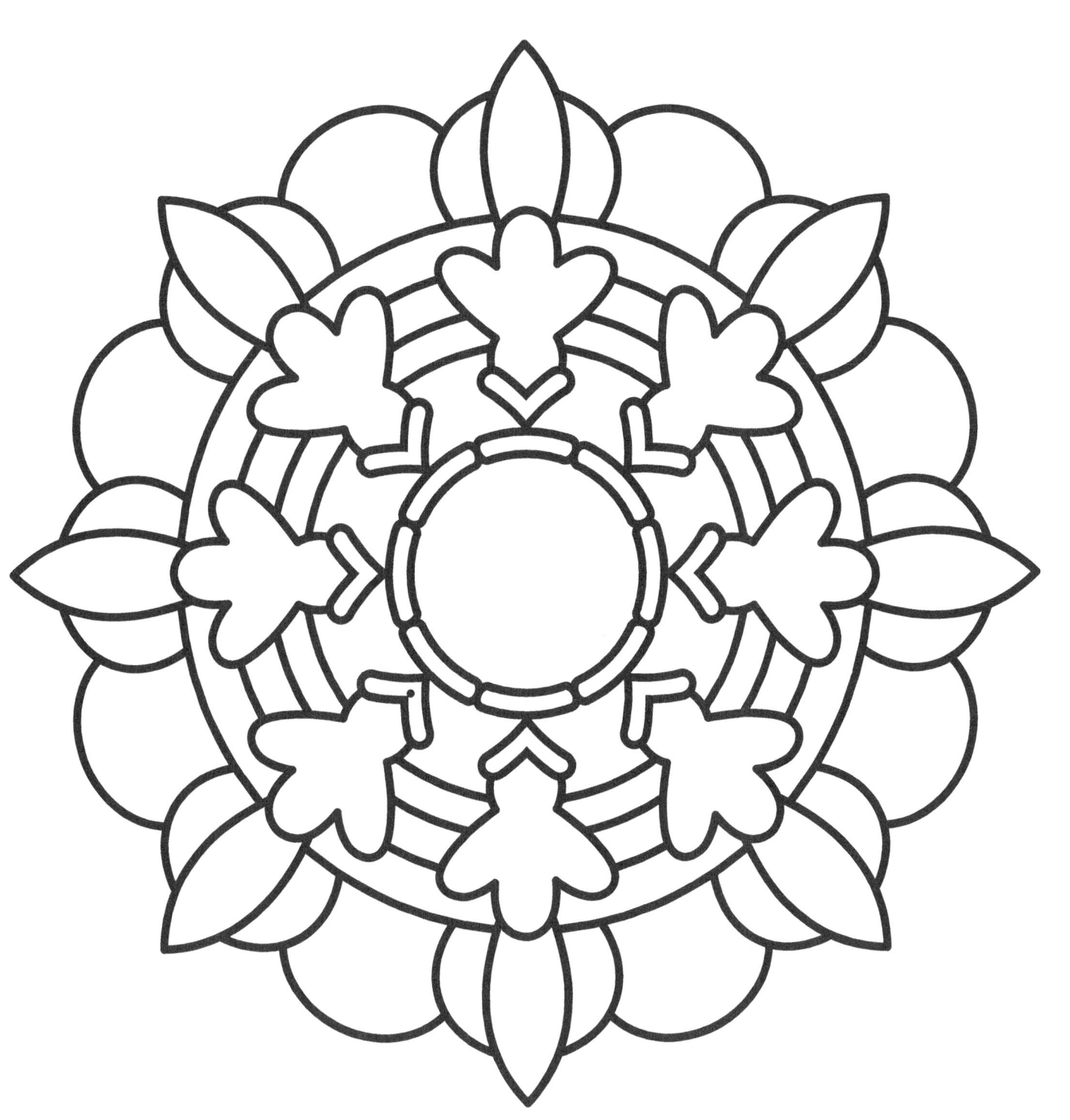

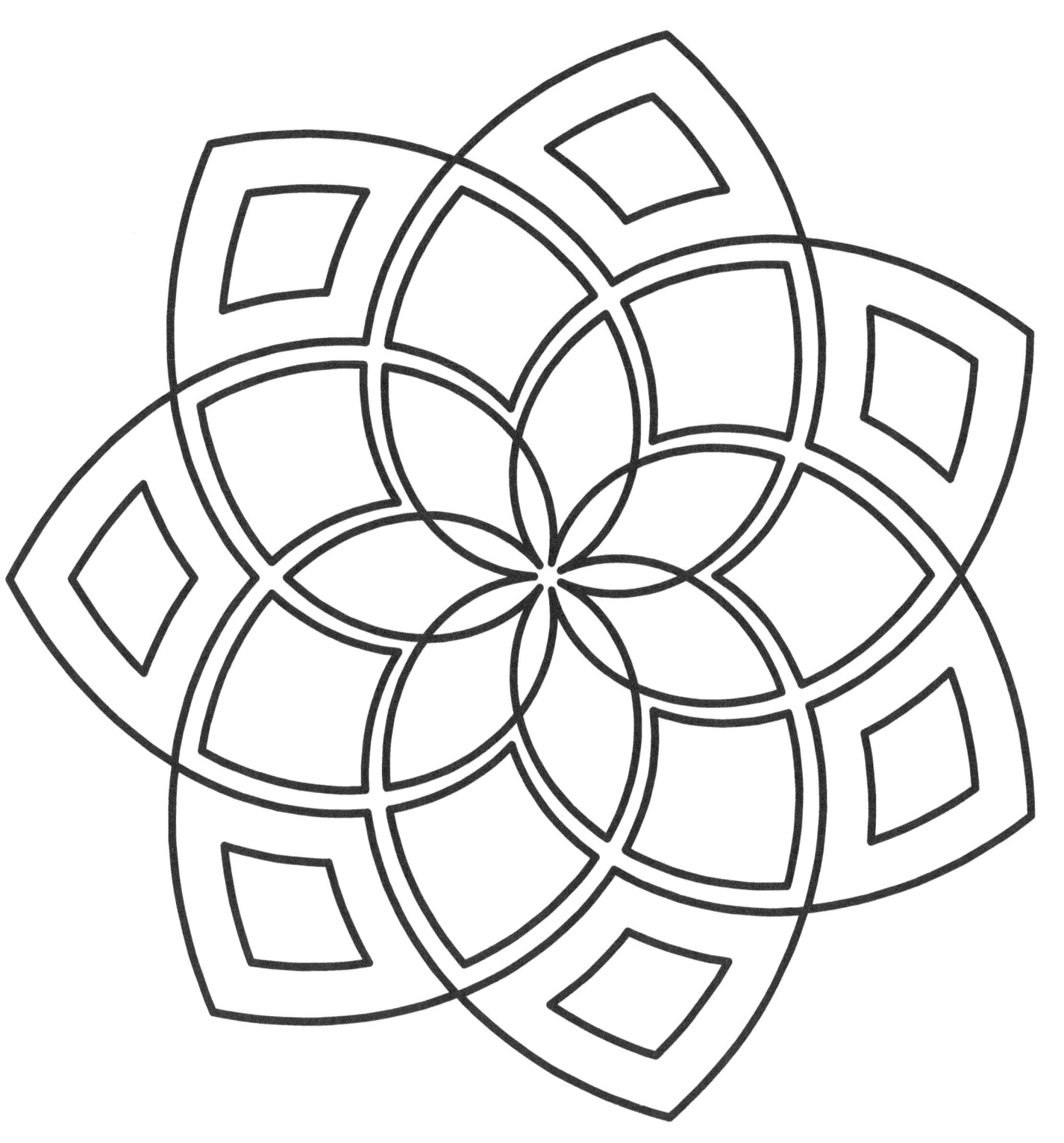

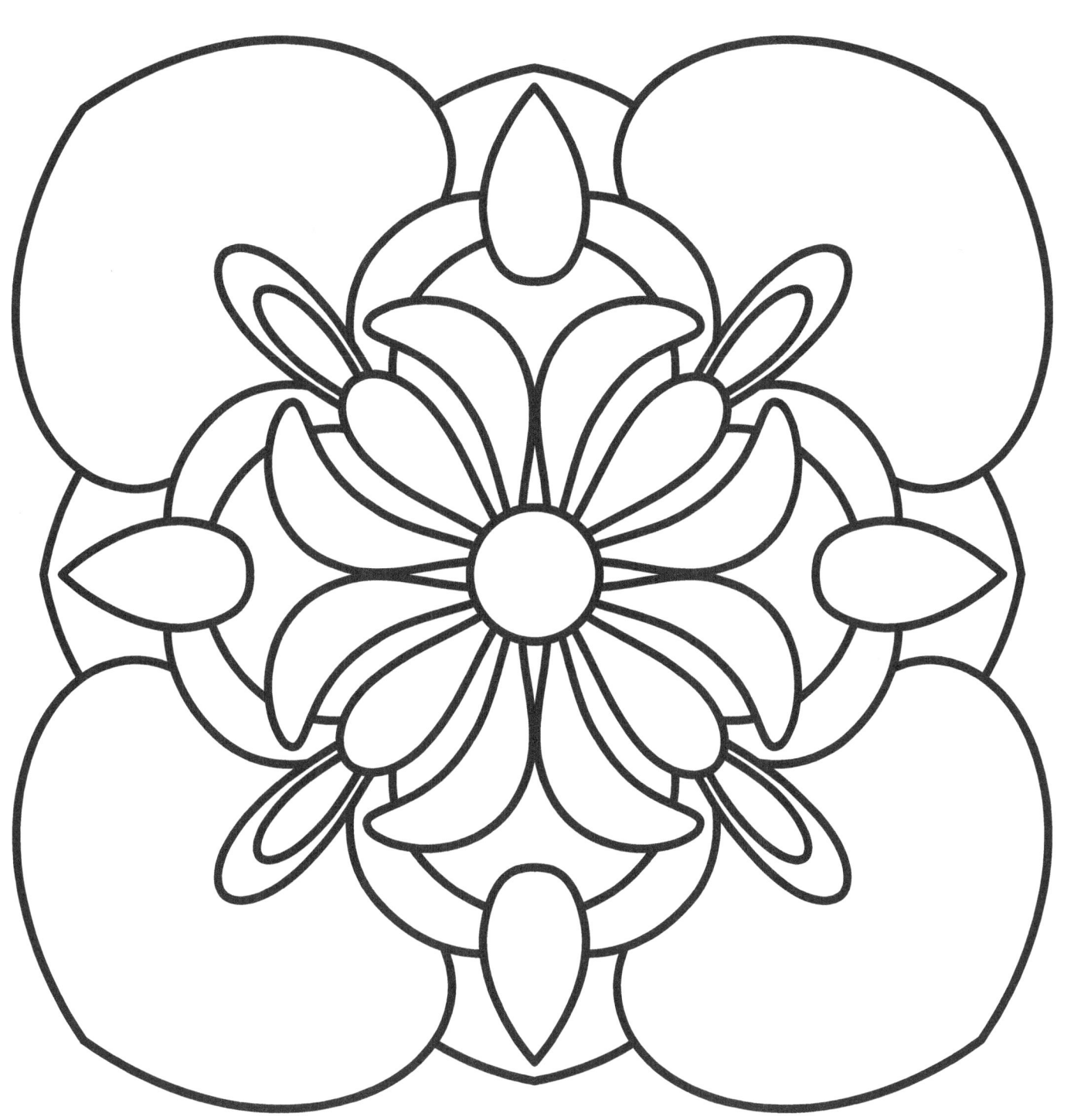

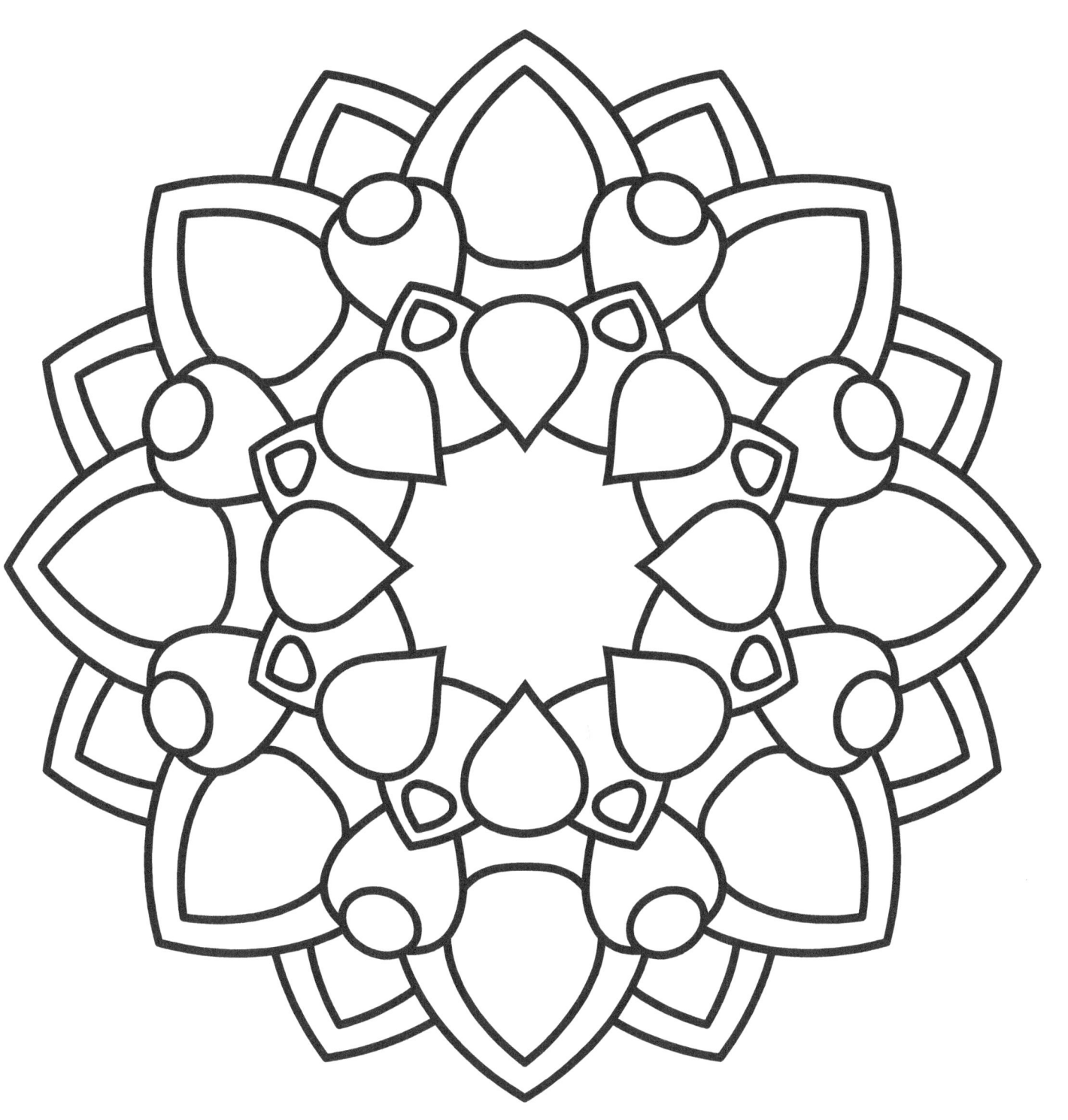

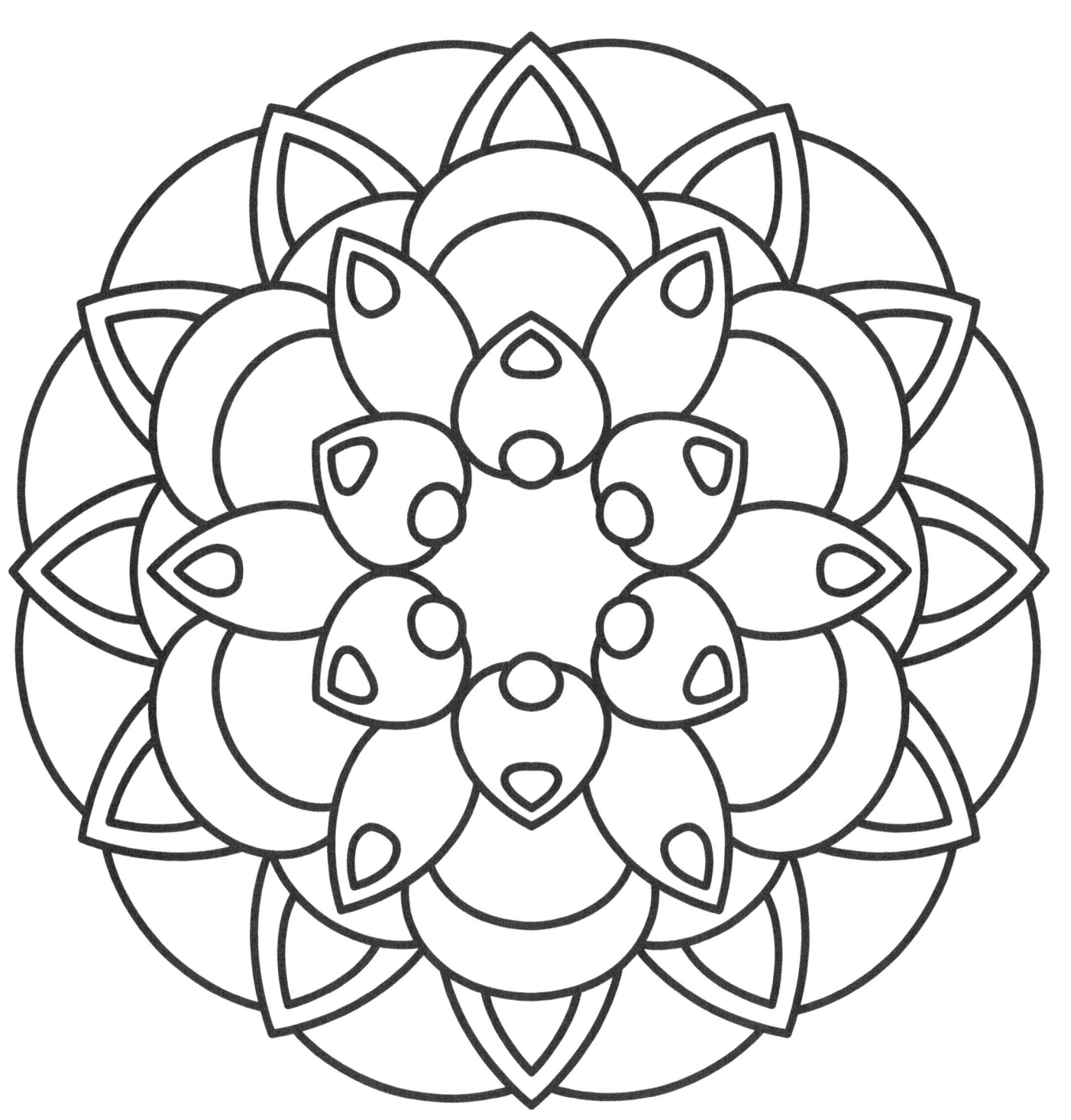

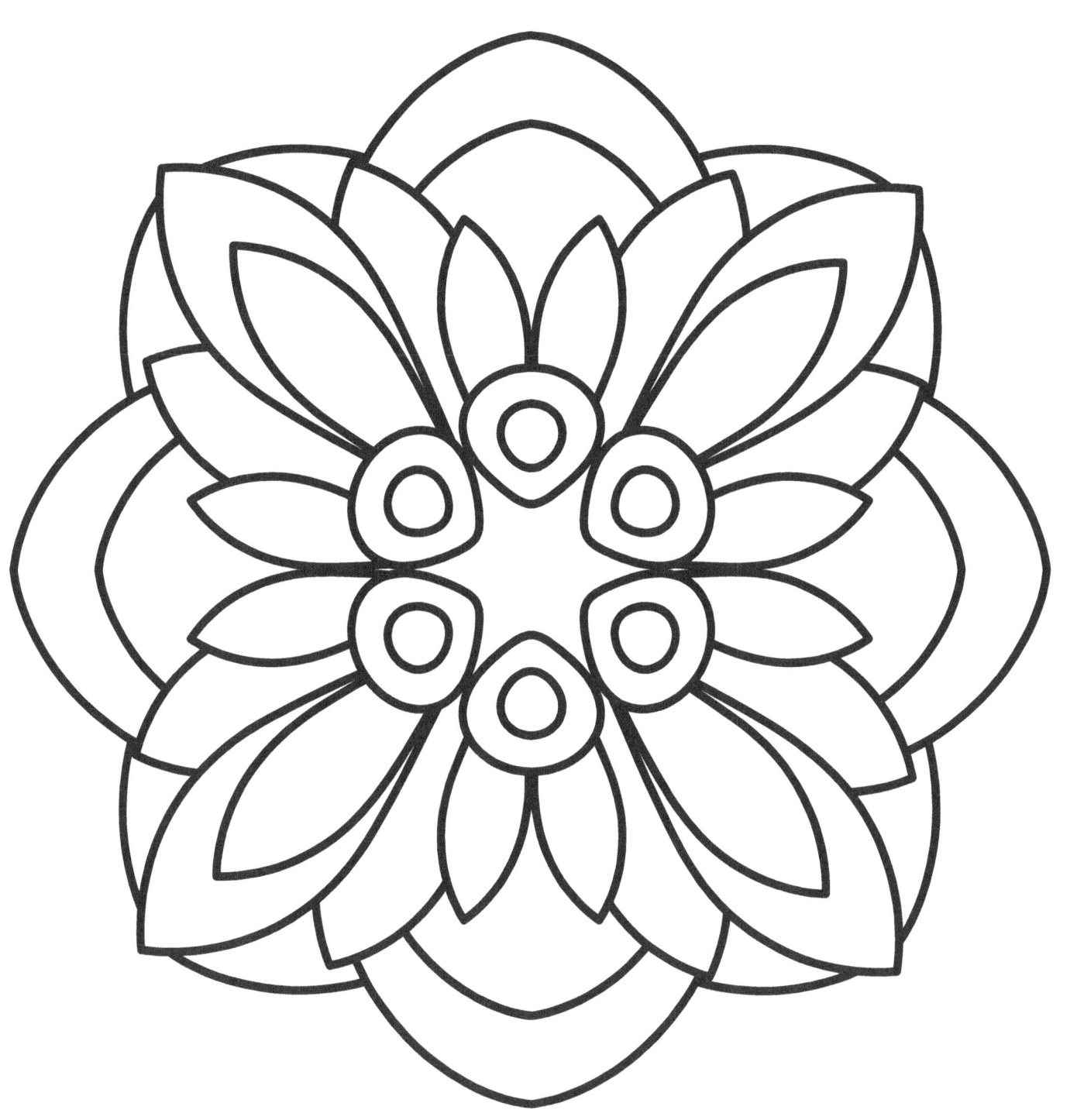

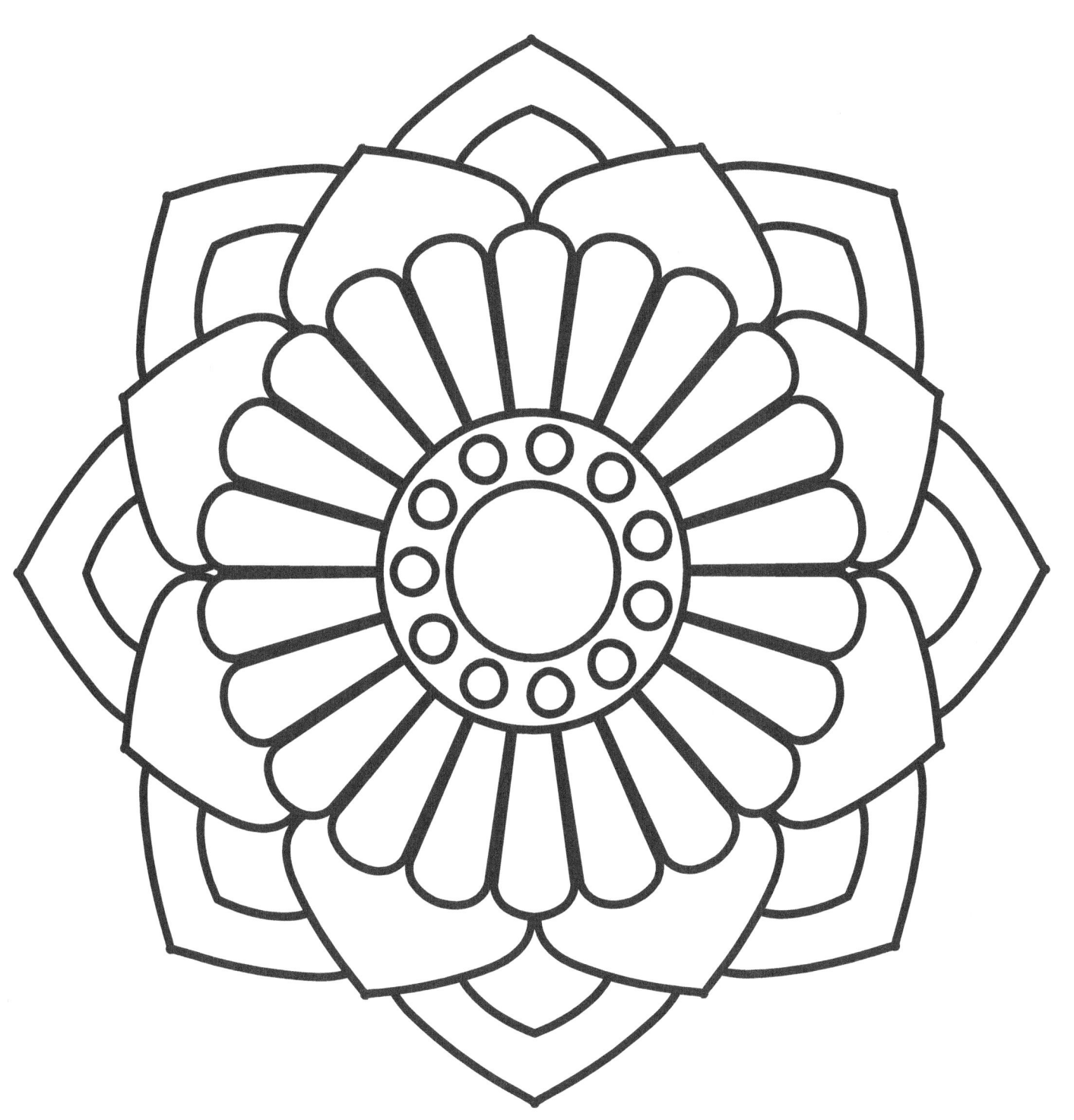

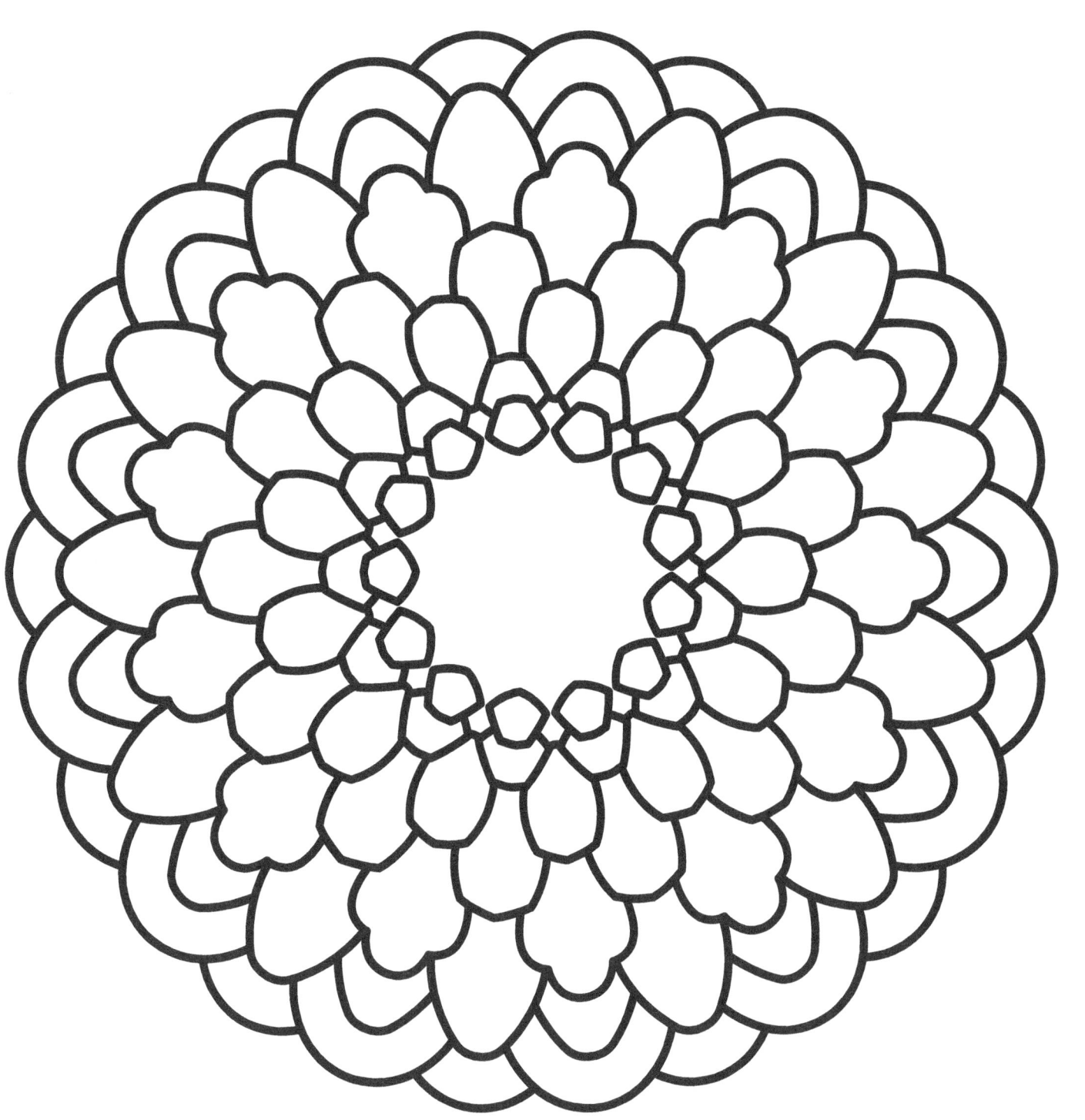

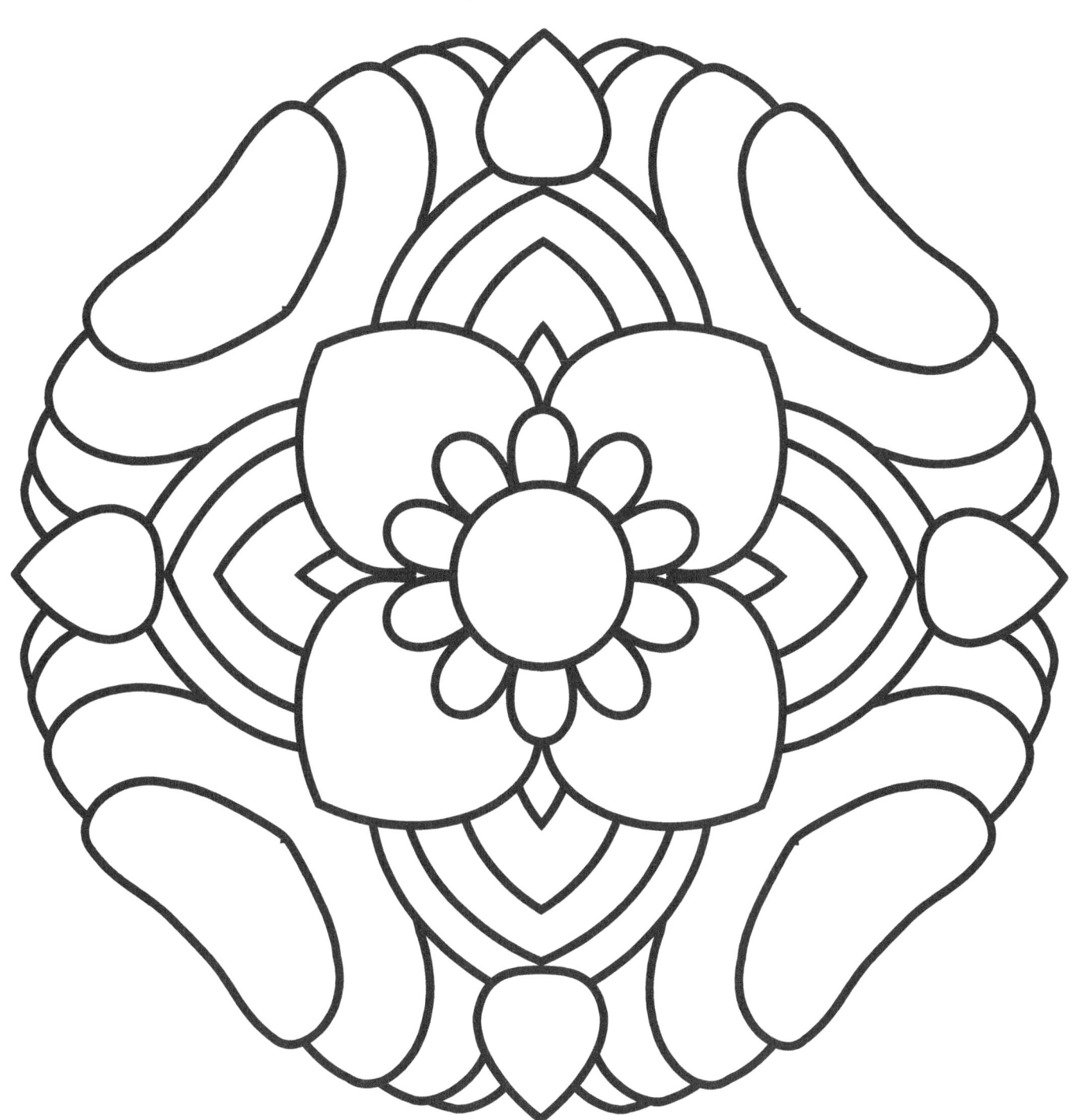

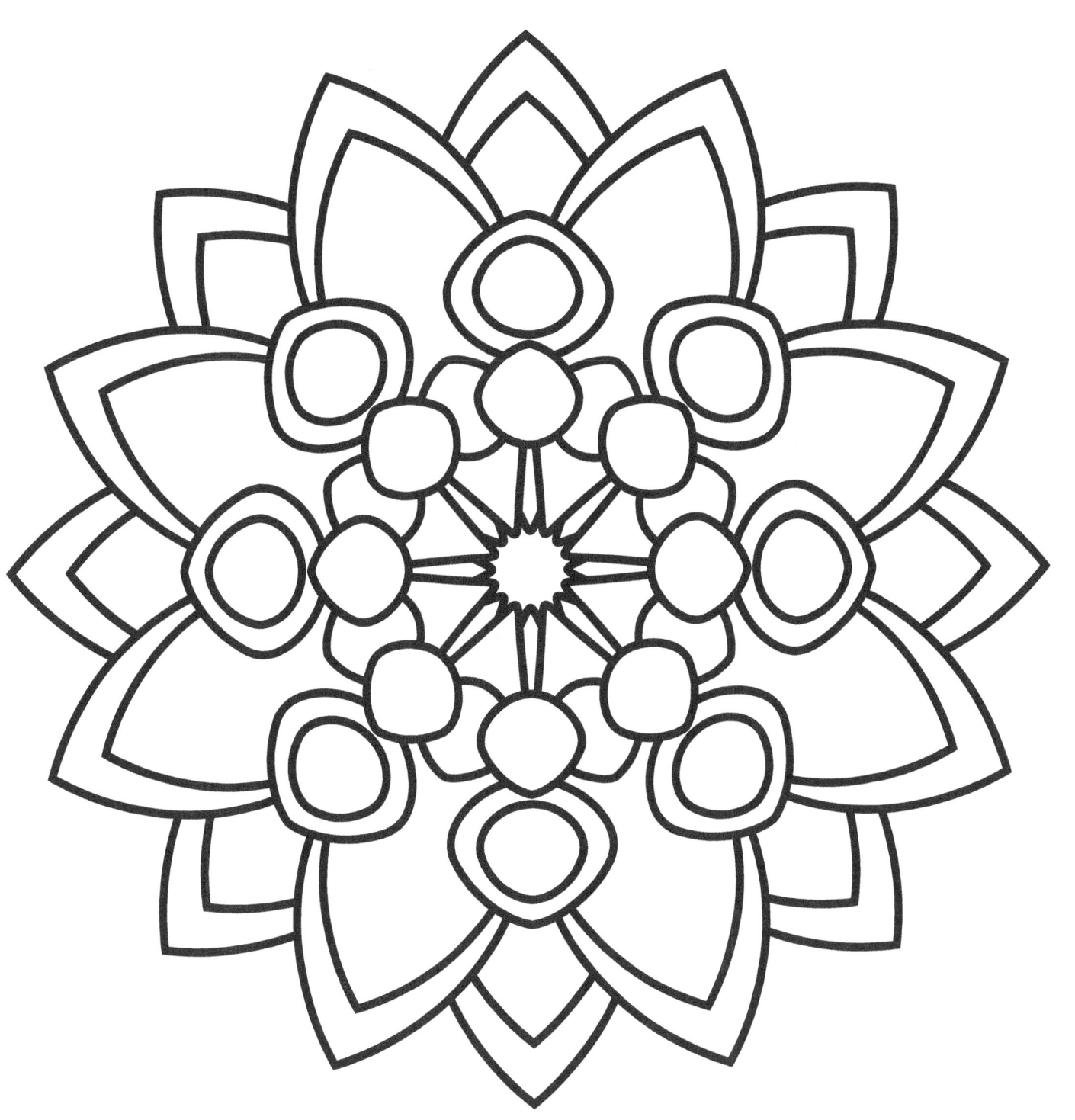

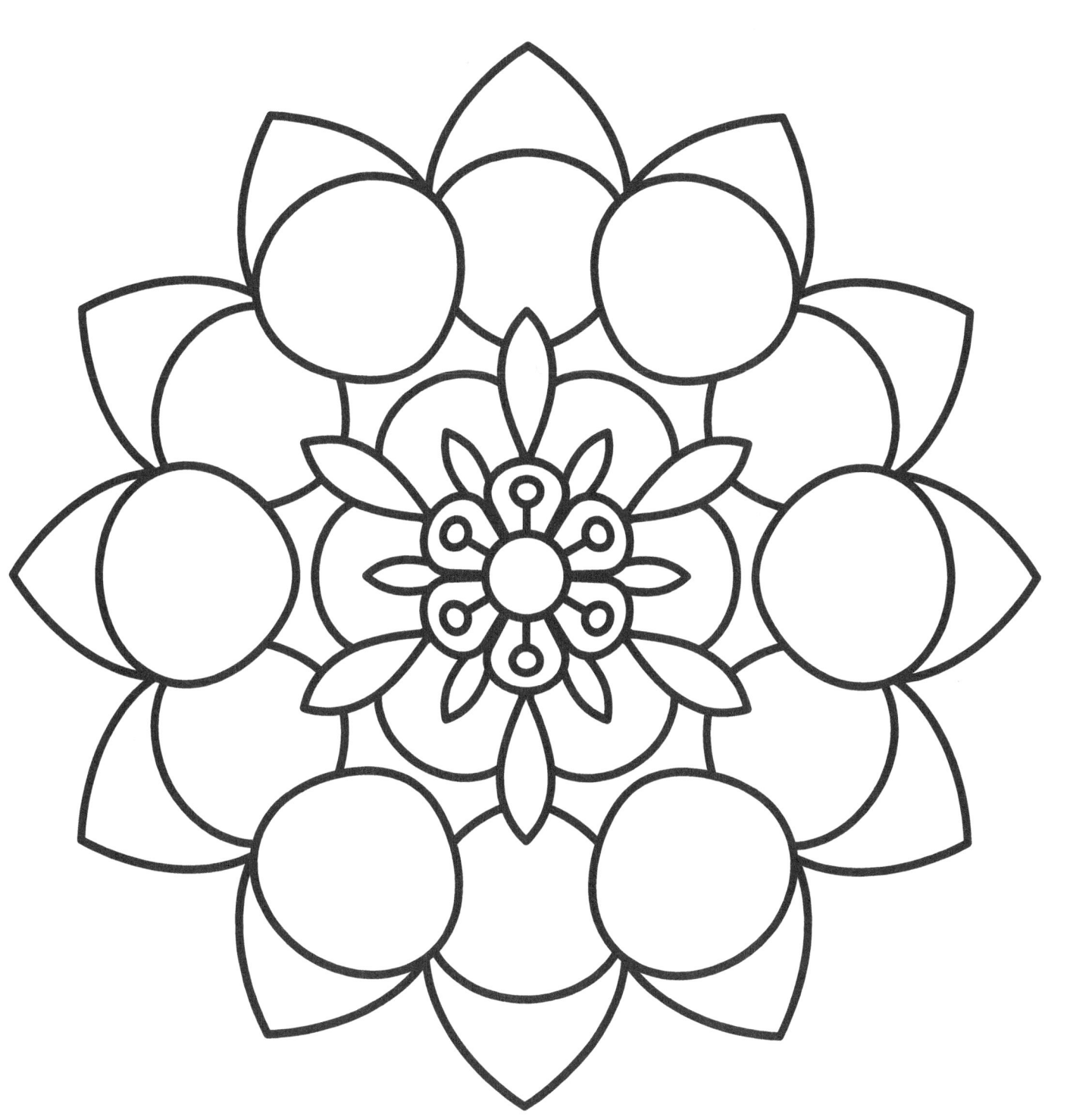

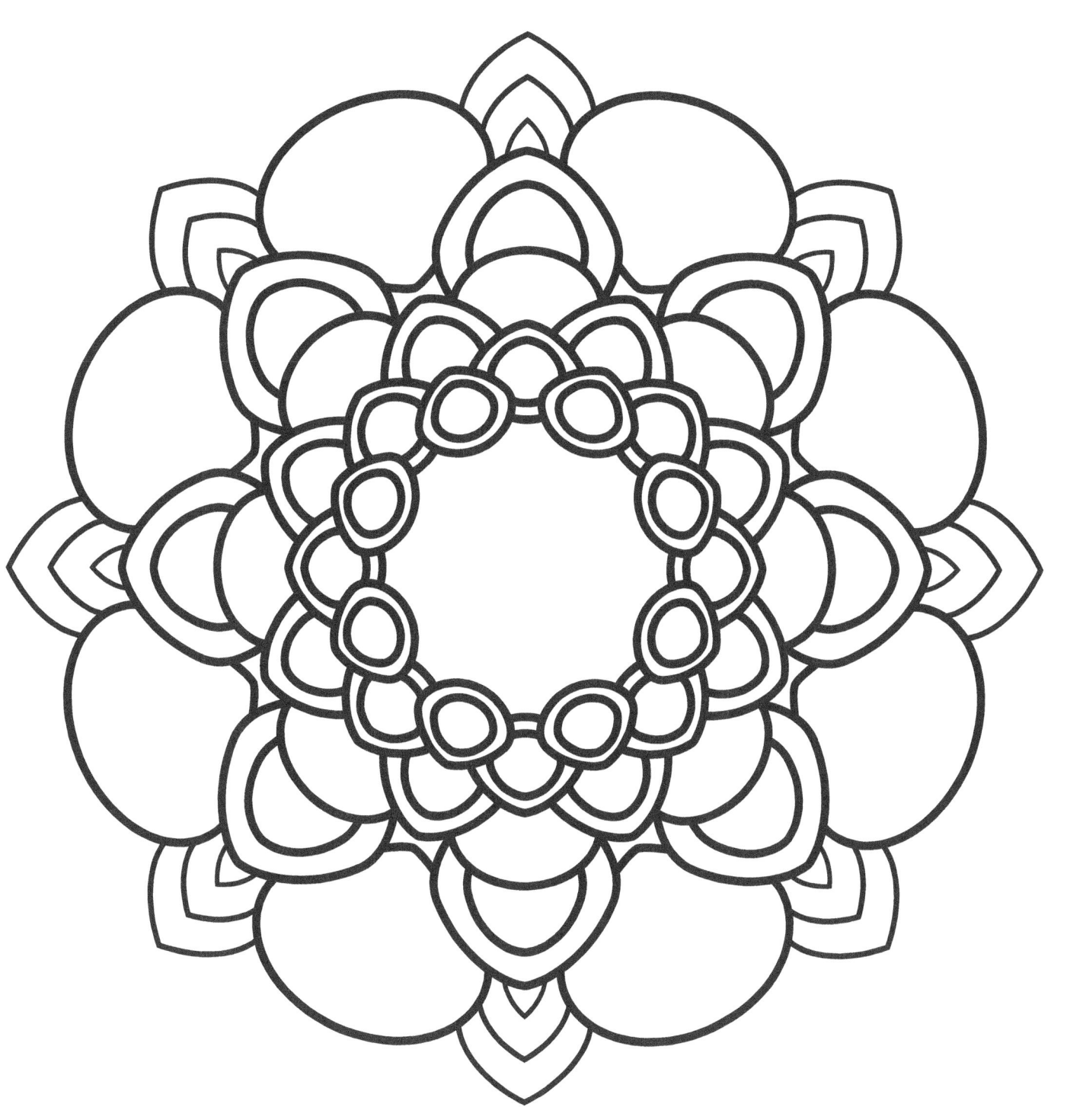

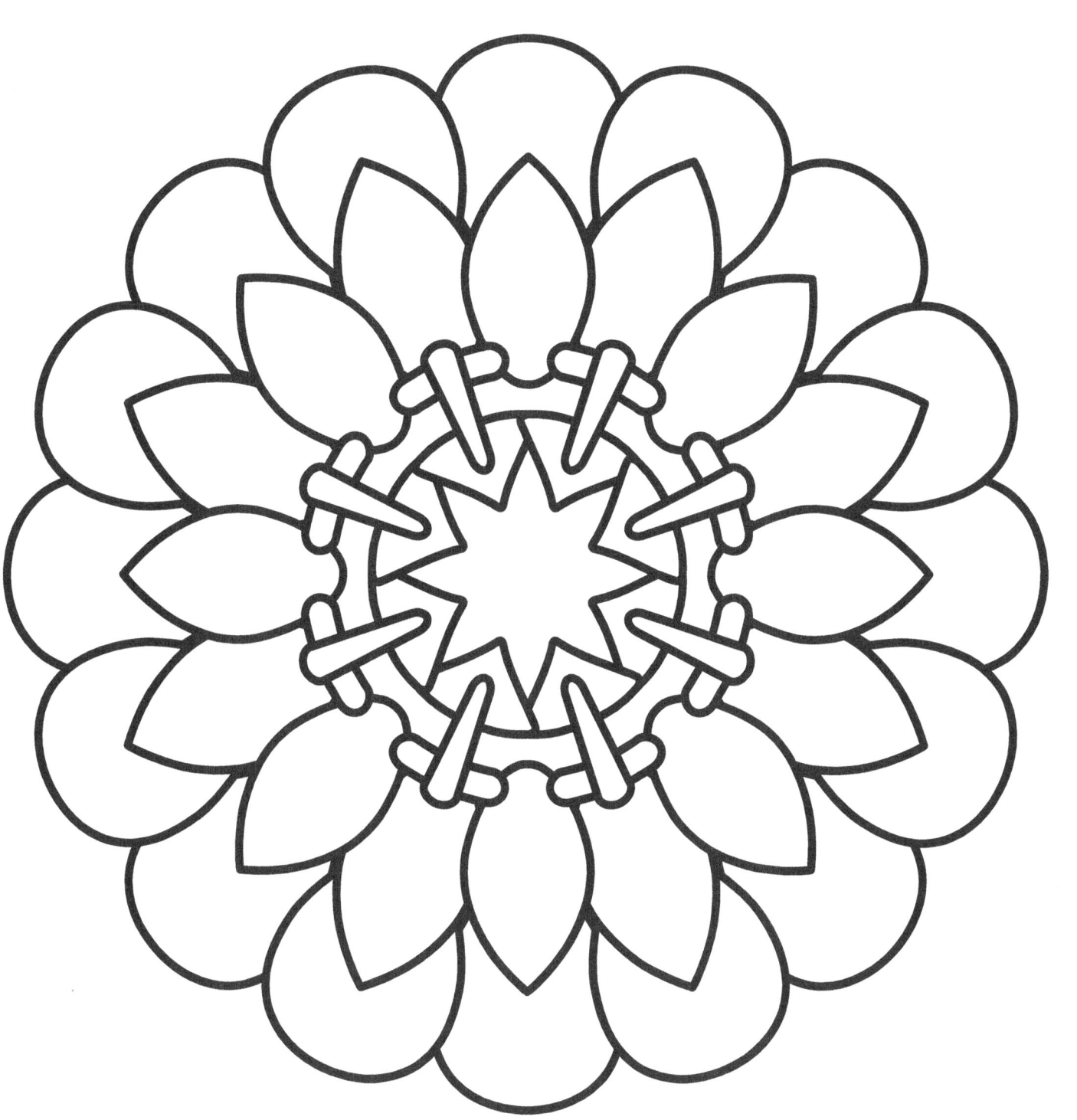

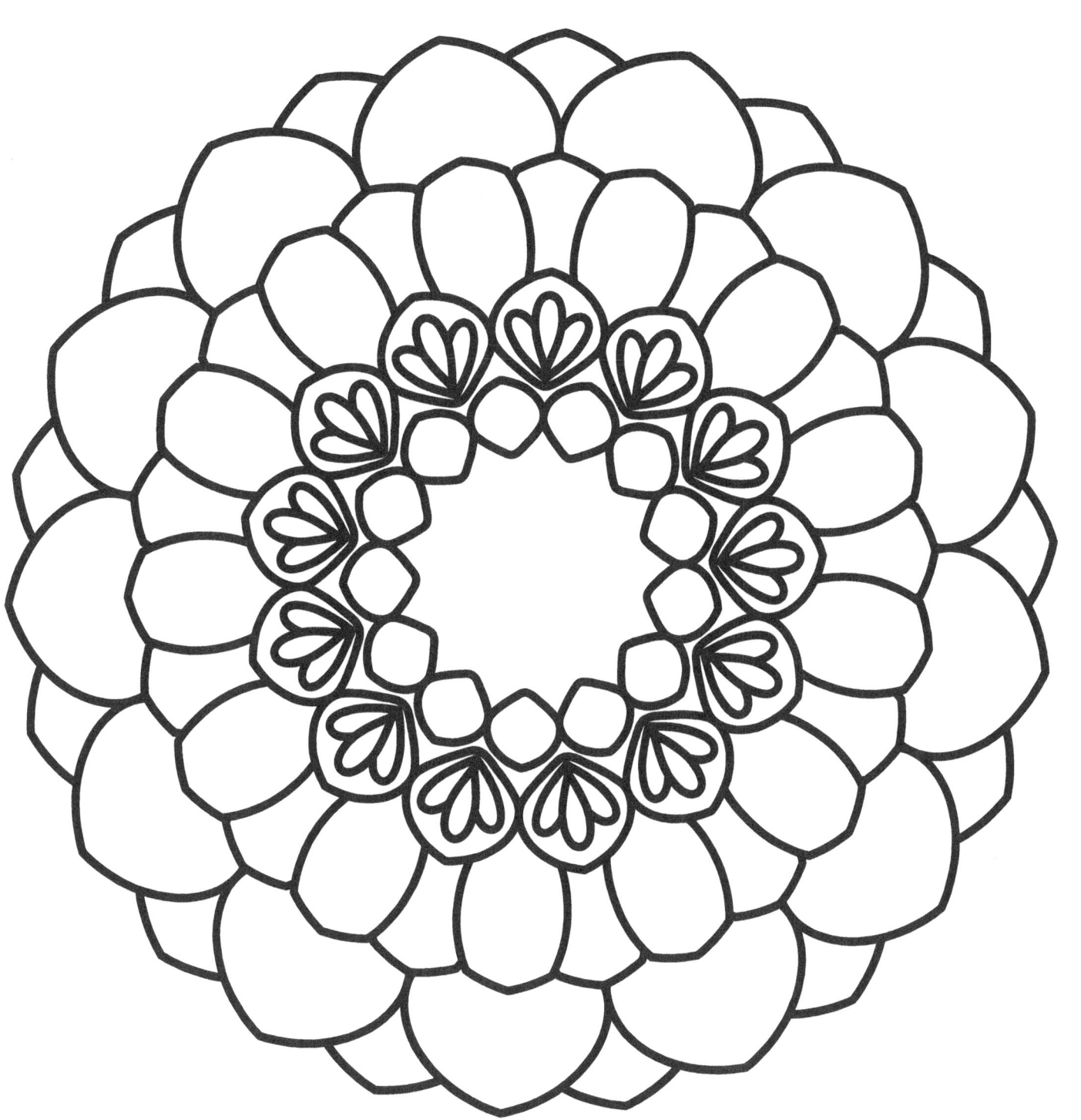

I'm very grateful to you, my dear Colorist, for choosing this coloring book and I hope you will enjoy every page of it as much as I did while creating it. Every single page was created with love and positive vibes of classic music.

Thank you for supporting my art-work. I would really appreciate if you could leave a **little feedback (review)** to encourage me to keep up a good work and to grow further as an artist.

BONUS: FULL DIGITAL VERSION OF THIS BOOK :)

Input this link **https://goo.gl/6YDZ1z** into your web browser (pay an attention to upper case letters). It will lead you to Dropbox-cloud-platform to get a Digital Version of this book in PDF format file. Just tap "Download" button and you'll have it on your PC for free. All Mandalas are on a regular white background and can be printed as a one file, in small groups or just one by one.

In case you'll have a problem with this file or the will to contact me directly, please write me an email to: **dv.design15@gmail.com**

I wish you to have a great time with this book :)

Sincerely yours, Elinorka.

www.ingramcontent.com/pod-product-compliance
Lightning Source LLC
Chambersburg PA
CBHW062225220526
45471CB00009B/3352

www.ingramcontent.com/pod-product-compliance
Lightning Source LLC
Chambersburg PA
CBHW062225220526
45471CB00009B/3352